PRAISE FOR WORTHY

Worthy is a big warm hug, a personal coaching session and a practical game plan all rolled into one. Sometimes, we need a reminder that we are worthy, and this book will help you rediscover your value and show you how to capitalise on it.

Leah Mether, speaker, trainer, coach, facilitator and author of the award-winning book, **Soft is the new hard: How to communicate effectively under pressure**

Before reading *Worthy*, I believed my introverted personality and 'nice' qualities as a leader were reasons to hold back my career progression. However, Maree McPherson taught me the value in how I lead and, indeed, how that makes me worthy of my achievements.

Ange Kasprowicz, assistant store manager, Target Australia

Few authors write from the heart like Maree McPherson. Written with deep insight, humility and strength, *Worthy* is for women who have spent their lives putting others before themselves and who dare to want more. This practical book will lift you up and give you the confidence to step into discomfort *your way* knowing you're in safe hands. Packed with simple activities, brilliant questions and real-life examples, *Worthy* is a must-read.

Kate Christiansen, award-winning author of The thrive cycle *and* Curly conversations for teams

To tackle worthiness for women is such an ambitious undertaking, and Maree McPherson has stepped up with her skills and experience to do the task justice. Many of us were conditioned to diminish ourselves and put others first, so looking deeply at our inherent worth can be uncomfortable. Maree points this out early and uses many stories of other women she has coached to help build understanding and insight. As a regional woman, Maree understands the comparisons we make of ourselves with our metro colleagues: our fear of being judged as lesser and our fear of tall poppy syndrome, which is rife in smaller communities. With her strategic prowess, Maree outlines an approach to self-investment and skill-building with a focus on what we actually want for ourselves, rather than proving something to others. *Worthy* provides a self-coaching tool and a manual for setting out an action plan to create the careers and fulfilment we deserve. It has helped me see where I am settling in my life and my career, and has provided me with steps to make changes to pursue that 'something more' that I want deep down. I know that it will have the same potential for you.

Jacqueline Brauman, principal solicitor, TBA Law

Like yoga, *Worthy* is a practice—one that allows us to be patient and human. Maree is generous with insights into creating a development budget and capitalising on your choices. Instead of striving for 'work-life balance', we are introduced to changing our life balance. What a revelation. I wish I had been gifted this book as a young woman. This book will show you how to model your values, which is important for those who are mentored by you.

Helen Robinett, leadership and confidence coach

In *Worthy*, Maree McPherson challenges and inspires us to find and step into our true worth, to take control of what we can, to live a life of great significance, and to create an enduring legacy for others. Maree calls on us to enter and stay in our courage zone, embrace ambition, maintain our mojo and commit to learning and growth. She provides practical guidance as to how to unlearn and become unstuck from unhelpful patterns that hold us back and keep us small. With elegance, grace, love and a dash of rebellion, Maree's words are at times gentle and assuring and, at others, unapologetically straight down the line. She challenges us to sit with discomfort, to persevere and to forge ahead. Thank you, Maree, for choosing to share this work with us as we step forward with renewed curiosity, connection and captivation.

Alison Coughlan, speaker, facilitator, coach and author of The health hazard: Take control, restore wellbeing and optimise impact

I've known Maree McPherson for nearly 20 years. I deeply respect and admire her talent to inspire a belief of worth in people. Maree achieves this through kindness, warmth, intelligence and integrity. An earnest yet powerful rhetorical prose is used to fuel purpose and stoke commitment. This is a book that jumps off the page in a series of parables used to hardwire the messages behind them in your mind. I am delighted to commend it as an engaging and relatable read.

Mary Aldred, CEO, Franchise Council of Australia, company director and winner of the Australian Financial Review BOSS Magazine *Young Executive of the Year 2018*

Worthy is truly powerful. Women of all ages and from all walks of life need to read this critically empowering message of deserved transformation. This book offers a plethora of insights as to why women should invest in themselves. It shows how building a life of meaning is closer than we think.

Kerryn Vaughan, speaker, facilitator, podcast host and award-winning author of Magnificent kids *and* Get off the bench: Kickstart your idea now

WHAT PEOPLE SAY ABOUT WORKING WITH MAREE

I have grown in confidence and experience, and I feel ready to take the next step. I have developed my toolkit of leadership resources that I will carry with me throughout my career.

Che Bishop, non-profit sector executive

I better understand my values and this means I have been able to grow my career in a way that benefits me, my family and my community.

Lisa Morgan, public sector program manager

I feel able to make decisions based on what's best for now, knowing I can circle back and reassess as the situation changes or develops. Although I haven't set goals, I know that isn't what I need. Maree reminded me that purpose motivates me, not targets.

Dr Charlie Aves, agribusiness executive officer

Maree is personable and extremely approachable, and she has a wonderful sense of humour. I found my energy levels were restored after my time with her. Her guiding questions inspired new ways of thinking and brought forth new ideas and strategies. This was a highlight in my leadership career.

Tracey Gibson, CEO, Prom County Aged Care

I undertook a coaching program with Maree. At the start of the program I felt lost and lacked confidence in my abilities. My goal was to find my authentic self again. Throughout the program with Maree, I noticed that she used gentle questioning techniques to help me delve into the root causes of my situation. Maree was patient and caring, and shared such valuable insights based on her own experiences. At the conclusion of our coaching sessions, I felt I had gained a whole new perspective on my strengths and abilities. I am now better equipped to be kinder to myself. I 100% recommend Maree for anyone wanting to raise the bar both personally and professionally.

Suzanne Thompson, Lean practitioner, project management, HR strategy, change management

WORTHY

WORTHY

Stop mauling your mojo; straighten your self-talk and create an intentional life

MAREE MCPHERSON

Copyright © Maree McPherson

All models copyright © Maree McPherson

First published in 2021 in Melbourne, Australia

ISBN: 978-0-646-84175-5

 A catalogue record for this book is available from the National Library of Australia

Edited by Joanna Yardley at The Editing House

Cover design and illustrations by Lacey Yeomans

Typeset, printed and bound in Australia by BookPOD

All rights reserved. No part of this publication may be reproduced by any means without the prior written consent of the publisher.

This book uses case studies to enforce the meaning behind its relevant chapter. Some names have been changed to protect individual privacy.

Every effort has been made to trace (and seek permission for use of) the original source of material used within this book. Where the attempt has been unsuccessful, the publisher would be pleased to hear from the author / publisher to rectify any omission.

Contents

	Foreword	xiii
	Preface	xv
	Acknowledgements	xvii
	About the author	xxiii
	Introduction	1
Chapter One	Self-development is not a luxury	7
Chapter Two	Why you can't wait	17
Chapter Three	Making money matters	27
Chapter Four	Don't I need another degree?	35
Chapter Five	But ambition isn't nice	47
Chapter Six	Connection builds capacity	57
Chapter Seven	Hit the road, Jill	71
Chapter Eight	Leadership is lonely, isn't it?	83
Chapter Nine	Commitment and clarity	95
	Conclusion	105
	References	109

Foreword

I grew up in the north of England in the Thatcher years and stiff upper lip class system. I was always told that my work should speak for itself. I was told to be humble and keep quiet about the things I was achieving. I was constantly told, 'Keep your head down and do not in any way call attention to yourself'.

The result for me (as it is for many others) is that I became invisible as I languished behind the scenes, taking a back seat and not getting noticed. I wasn't brave enough to speak up, to step into the spotlight or to stand out in any way. In those early years it meant I was overlooked for promotions and opportunities.

Thirteen years ago, everything changed—personally and professionally. I had three young children; I was experiencing corporate bullying at a senior level; and I was working way more than I was playing. I was stuck, lost, uncertain and simply existing on the treadmill of life.

Like many, I was tackling the ongoing and exhausting battle between striving for more and proving I was good enough. 'Mother guilt' was a constant companion. I felt alone. And despite rising through the ranks, self-doubt always told me I wasn't smart enough, savvy enough, brave enough or good enough to be there. I decided enough was enough and it was time to take ownership of my life and my career. It was time to make the right choices for me and to get back in the driving seat of my life.

The business I was with at the time didn't invest in executive coaches, so I dug deep and made that investment myself—after all, something had to change. To say that this decision changed my career and my life beyond anything I'd ever dreamt is an understatement, but that is a story for another time.

Discovering my worth, and unlocking my voice, my dreams and my confidence to play a different and bigger game, allowed me to truly discover who I was, who I was being and, ultimately, who I wanted to become.

Maree's book is a game changer for any woman wanting to achieve more, be more and live more. Her insights, smarts and experience combined with many practical exercises are the tools we all need to become our brilliant selves so that we can each leave the impact we want for our families, teams, clients and communities. It's time to become the worthy woman you already are.

Janine Garner
International speaker and 3x bestselling author
committed to connecting with and helping women
around the planet to unlock their brilliant selves

Preface

A confession. I'm a bit of an overachiever and a perfectionist—a professional development addict. Despite achieving some great things in my life, I've had a few false starts along the way, and in this book, I will share what I learned from those setbacks.

After a 35-year career in regional and metropolitan Australia, I founded my own leadership development company, The Grass Ceiling, where I help leaders thrive and organisations form legacies.

You could say I'm obsessed with creating fulfilling opportunities for women in regional Australia. Because I am one and always have been.

Worthy draws on my coaching of more than 100 regional leaders over hundreds of hours, stories from women in my workshops over the past seven years, and the many managers in my development programs with Australian companies. My clients include leading regional organisations and ambitious individuals.

I know that people sometimes lose their love for their work. I have learned what causes this loss. My job is to create a safe space for exploration and growth so people can use their insights to create impact and thrive with a renewed sense of purpose. As you read this book, you can expect me to stretch your thinking but not so hard that it snaps. I'll also help you stay accountable for the change you want to achieve by summarising each chapter with exercises to do, articles to read or questions to answer.

I will describe the most common challenges women face when investing in their learning and personal growth. I'll discuss how to circumvent these challenges and step over the hurdles. There are practical tools and stories from women who had insights into their blockers and shifted them.

Before you read on, I want you to prepare to feel unsettled. I need you to open your mind and be curious about what's possible. Be ready to tap into what you already know, even though it's hidden from you right now. Please also be willing to hold yourself in high regard; this is essential for readers of this book. If you can do those things, you will get the maximum benefit.

I want you to find the job you love or to fall back in love with the job you have. I want to help you make the best use of your precious time and funds by targeting the learning and development you desire most. And if you find yourself wondering about a leadership role in the future, but you think you might be under-equipped or that you will feel too isolated, I'll teach you how to connect for capacity-building so you can lean into leadership.

However, if everything in your career is hunky-dory, put this book back on the shelf. If you've bought it, gift it to someone who needs it, or save it for the day when your mojo eludes you and you're wondering how you slipped so far down your own priority list that you are ranked the lowest.

Acknowledgements

An author's job is not complete until they have thanked the people who inspired them to write and finish a book. So, here goes.

Thanks to my parents for ensuring I completed my school education and urging me on to my first university studies. You kept a safe roof over my head, food in my belly, fuel in my car, and filled the pantry of my first house when I moved out. I owe you both so much.

To my husband of 30 years, Warren. Thanks for seeing me through book number two. You know I love to write, and I know that your constant supply of cups of tea, back rubs, hugs, and your best pasta dishes and curries have got us to here. Thank you for inspiring me and telling me I was on track. You helped more than you could ever know.

To the women who volunteered to be interviewed for the book—thank you for your contributions and your patience. Without these women, *Worthy* might never have been written. When I interviewed these women in 2019, my idea was to write a book about mentoring. I recorded their interviews, prepared transcripts, and hunkered down to write. Then, my father died and I spent a good long time unable to write as I grieved.

When I came back to the book in September 2020, I knew it had to be different. No longer about mentoring alone, it became the book you are reading now. An international pandemic and numerous lockdowns helped me recall stories and focus on experiences that enriched my writing. It seems every cloud has a silver lining after all.

I simply would not be at the point of publishing without the assistance of my book coach, Kath Walters. Kath helped me bring *Worthy* to life with her methodology, encouragement, clarity of thought, and her kindness. Kath, your support enabled me to stay the course. Sharing this with you and my book buddy, Jacqui Alder, has been a pleasure.

A huge virtual hug to my dear friend, Kate Anderson. Kate is the founder and owner of Indispensable Me—a boutique business in Melbourne. Kate offered me her services as an indispensable person prepared to come on board and conduct an early literature review. Readers will see her work scattered throughout the pages of the book. Thank you, Kate.

Clients are the lifeblood of my practice. Without all of you, there would be no stories to share, no 'aha' moments or fist-pumping successes. I truly cherish the way you allow me into your lives and the transformations you show me.

Special thanks to my first readers, Leah, Suzanne, Jodie, and darling Ange. Your generous comments and suggestions helped shape *Worthy* and I am forever grateful.

Thanks to my editor, Joanna Yardley from The Editing House. Jo, I selected you based on the wonderful job you did editing my first book. But it was more than that. When you edited my inaugural blog in 2016, we established a trust and rapport that remains. I knew *Worthy* would be safe in your capable and caring hands.

Lacey Yeomans, my practice manager, you make my world a better place. We have known each other for a long time now, and we share a virtual world that, simply, works. Thank you for the beautiful cover design and illustrations, and for being you.

There is a long list of champions who have helped me in my practice. That list is too long to add here. There are, however, two special mentors I wish to acknowledge. Linda Hutchings planted the first seeds of *Worthy* when she encouraged me to write my second book. I still have the handwritten A4 page of notes from a conversation with you when we spoke via Zoom from your home in New Zealand. Big love, Linda.

I also want to recognise Janine Garner for her mentoring. Janine, you saw something in me from our earliest conversations, and you have helped me to find my brilliance. Thank you. The best is yet to come.

To my best friends and to all my family—growing larger by the year. Thank you for loving me; that's the best gift of all. I love you back ... and you're all worth it.

For Jan Grassens

September 1933–January 2020

Dad, you were so proud of my first book, *Cutting through the grass ceiling*. I wish I could see your beaming smile with the publication of *Worthy*. Thank you for urging me to be the best version of me, always.

A great father is a lifelong gift and I will relish that gift for the rest of my days.

Peace be with you.

About the author

With a strong belief that impact follows insight, Maree McPherson's gifts bring organisations to life through what she sees, hears and feels. Maree helps develop organisations into legacies by assisting people to think and make sense of what they discover.

Maree's leadership experience spans over 35 years and includes a chief executive role in a peak body and another in a regional development organisation. Initially trained in social welfare, Maree started her career in case management with children's services.

Now her clients include ambitious individuals and leading organisations. Maree has worked with individual leaders and leadership teams within organisations to embrace lifelong learning and create a legacy. Her proven strategy revolves around helping leaders thrive at work by teaching them how to deliver the clarity that drives certainty.

With postgraduate level training in executive and organisational coaching and business management, Maree is a renowned coach and consultant facilitator in Australia.

She is one of the 4.1% of coaches in Australia and New Zealand serving as a member of the International Coaching Federation—the largest professional coach membership and credential-providing body globally. Maree works within the professional ethics and guidelines designated by both the International Coaching Federation and the Standards Australia HB 332-2011 for Coaching in Organisations. Maree is also a member of the

Association for Coaching. She is an accredited practitioner in the Mayer-Salovey-Caruso Emotional Intelligence Test (MSCEIT).

Introduction

Andie (not her real name) sat with me at a dinner event in 2018. We had never met and we got talking. It wasn't long before Andie described how she felt stuck and under-appreciated. The team who reported to her didn't seem to listen to her directions. She thought her team wasn't performing. Yet it was something else that was eating away at her. Andie had lost her love of work and she wanted more.

Everything about Andie's language told me she regretted not having acted on this sooner. Andie felt it was too late. Her children were in their teens; her partner earned good money and her income was excellent. On the surface, Andie had a life other women would envy. Yet she felt shallow, bored and listless. She sighed a lot.

Andie told me her children came first in all her decisions. She had made a career out of putting her own needs last—even as far back as leaving school earlier than planned. Andie's parents had owned a small business supplying the agricultural sector. Cash flow had been affected by years of drought and floods. So, to save her parents from any further financial stress, Andie got a job rather than going on to university.

Andie was concerned about the role model she was being for her teenage daughter. To quote Andie,

'This is what women do, love. We put everyone else's needs before our own. We put our dreams on hold while we get everyone else sorted'.

Andie knew this wasn't what she wanted but didn't know how to change it.

Andie told me how she imagined herself in her own business, finding her place as a community leader, and using some of her revenue to support a local charity. All this information came tumbling out in a 30-minute conversation with a perfect stranger who was willing to listen and not judge her.

Andie was embarrassed and tearful at having been so forthright and vulnerable. She excused herself, finished her meal and left the event. I knew then that I had to help Andie and the many women I had met who were just like her.

My mother, the most important female role model in my life, had a story similar to Andie's. Mum had wanted to become a mothercraft nurse. She attended a small rural school where students finished at the equivalent of today's year eight. Mum tried correspondence education, but it was too tricky being so remote from all of her teachers.

Mum left school to start work as a bookkeeper, moving to retail sales before starting her family. By the age of 23, mum had three children under six. Her fourth child (me) arrived when the eldest was nine.

Mum stayed home to rear us because that was the firm expectation of society in her generation. Mum always knew she had more to give. She volunteered as a Cub Scout leader, then went back to full-time work at the local hospital, initially as a cleaner. Mum was then afforded the opportunity to become a theatre technician. It was a role that sparked her curiosity and made more of her talent at the end of her working life.

My mother didn't have the options women have today. I want to honour her by ensuring as many women as possible capitalise on their choices.

If you are like Andie, if you identify with her story and if you are fearful of regrets, this book is for you. I'll show you how to decrease your boredom and increase your contentment, change your life balance and ensure you model your values to the people you love.

I'll also show you how to increase your options by investing a percentage of your income in your growth each year, then leveraging that investment to position yourself for a better salary and increased benefits. Many of my clients have already done this.

I want you to know that you are worthy. You are worthy of investing time, effort and money in your development and your future contentment. You're not only working to support your family or just to help your children meet their aspirations. It is *your* life. I want you to have a lifestyle with latitude and to experience the freedom that comes from flexibility.

Defining worthy and wistful words

> 'What a liberation to realise that the "voice in my head" is not who I am.'
>
> Eckhart Tolle

When my niece read the first draft of this book, she asked me a powerful question. She queried whether there was a moment in my life when I realised my worth and what it meant to me. This was an excellent and insightful question (figures … she *was* raised by my big sister).

I know I was influenced by my parents wanting their children to have more prosperity and opportunities than themselves. My father often reminded his four children that we could be whatever we wanted to be as long as we strived to be as good as we could in our chosen job. It was important to strive for success and to have self-belief.

I also know there have been times when I have followed what seemed like good advice or where I have chosen a path because everyone else appeared to be on the same journey.

I learned that following my gut instincts worked out better for me than following the crowd. I can recognise times when the voice in my head (the one to which Tolle refers) seemed to define me. I was not enough unless I studied harder or gained more qualifications. I would have regrets if I didn't pursue a leadership job. I would forever kick myself if I turned down the opportunity to work in a state-wide executive role. I wouldn't have 'made it'.

My mentors were the people who helped me see that I was not the voice in my head— at least not the negative voice. School and university didn't give me that, but some teachers and one of my lecturers did. Several managers were influential, along with an executive coach who helped me unpack my blockers and act on my goals.

So, I know now that Tolle is right. **Your self-talk is not who you are**. However, it is helpful to understand how your self-talk affects your life decisions. Your wistful language is passive and based on an external locus of control. Wistful language keeps you small. Your inner voice leads you to feel insignificant and inconsequential.

This means you are more inclined to:

- Put your needs last and everyone else first.
- Focus on the cost of the things that matter to you.
- Risk making rash and ill-considered decisions.
- Self-censor.

In contrast, your worthy language is proactive and reflects an internal locus of control. This self-talk allows you to take up more space in the world, to feel influential and valuable.

Worthy thinking allows you to:

- Put your needs first without guilt.
- Focus on value and return on investment instead of cost.
- Optimise decisions by being well-informed and strategic.
- Self-validate.

> WORTHY
> PROACTIVE
> INTERNAL LOC

This book's premise is that you need to adopt worthy language and thoughts to help you stay focused on your lifelong learning objectives. Self-belief allows you to soar. Without it, you stall.

Before you read further, I need you to do an exercise. (It's not as challenging as it sounds.)

> **Exercise 1**
>
> On a page, create a table with two columns. Give the first column the header 'My Wistful Words' and the second column the header 'My Worthy Words'. Write as many words as possible in each column to reflect your self-talk, depending on how you feel.
>
> Keep your contrast frame handy as you read this book. Through each chapter, it will be a reminder of your thoughts and feelings.

Here's an example to help you.

My Wistful Words	My Worthy Words
Nostalgic: Thinking about how life was better when X.	Deserving: I deserve to have X.
Desiring: I used to want X.	Valuable: I am valuable because X (or I value X).
Sad: I missed out on X.	Model: When I do X, I'm modelling the person I want to be.

You might enjoy Christine Carter's TED Talk called *The 1-minute secret to forming a new habit*. Carter shows the importance of being prepared to flounder when you start something new.

This introduction shows how thinking affects our inner dialogue and why worthy words are better than wistful words. Don't expect to be perfect at worthy self-talk straight away—but don't give up. You can do this. Allow yourself days of low motivation and negative moments. You will progress with patience and practice.

CHAPTER ONE

Self-development is not a luxury

Women need to look after their own development needs. Having a career or job they want is not an indulgence. It starts with taking advancement seriously. When women stop envying their colleagues and friends, they get moving towards their goals—whether those goals are to secure the job of their dreams, a leadership role in the community, a better income, or something else.

Women ought to understand that self-development matters and it impacts their entire lives positively (not just their careers). When women put themselves first, they don't hesitate. When women don't do this, the risk is regret.

Some women who ignore lifelong learning become grudging employees and unhappy at home. They regret not being the role model they'd like to be for their children, friends and colleagues. Women with self-worth know learning is not a luxury. They prioritise their growth. They see themselves as worthy.

In this chapter, I'll discuss why your family's needs are essential but not more important than your own. I'll ask you to stop envying your friends with assumed better lives because your envy is mauling your mojo. I'll also discuss why this leads to a balanced life.

Meet your needs

On an aeroplane, the flight safety check is the flight crew's first task after all passengers are seated and the plane is taxiing. Flight attendants instruct passengers to put their masks on first before assisting other people. They show passengers how the oxygen mask will drop and ask them to ensure their safety as a priority.

Likewise, when women make learning a focus, they help their careers and others, including their families. I intend to convince women that their own needs are just as important as their children's or partner's.

The women I coach tell me the role models they had as children are not the role models they want to be for others. Putting others first (service above oneself) and demonstrating love is admirable but there are costs.

One client told me she chooses to work part-time to be home each afternoon when her children come home from school. There's nothing wrong with that. She's proud of how she puts her children first even though she wants to work more hours. Yet she's often unwell and wrestles with the sense of not being as accomplished in her career as she would like to be. She feels like she is in a double bind and cannot talk to anyone else about it. What do you think is happening here? I have a hunch that she would like to expand herself professionally but sees this as a betrayal of her role as a good parent. Tricky.

Society expects women to be carers and nurturers. Women have interpreted this (with lots of help, I might add) as putting themselves last. Even if this isn't explicit, those implicit messages and social pressures can make women feel guilty.

Alice Eagly, professor of psychology at Northwestern University, and Steven Karau, professor of management at Southern Illinois University, studied prejudice towards female leaders. Their research showed that a lack of strong role models for women perpetuates an entrenched sense of the way things are supposed to be. From early life, women are accustomed to seeing men at the top of families, organisations, and nations—as in, it's normal for men to be in charge. Eagly and Karau found that when we see a departure from the norm, men and women can experience incongruence in their role.

Is it any wonder some of us find it hard to allow our dreams to take precedence?

Some women believe these debates belong in the past. Feminism has fixed things, surely? Recall the conversations you've had with your mother, grandmothers or other significant influencers in your life. What did those women say they regretted most or wish they had done? Think about the impact their words had on you as a child, a teenager, and in adulthood. Is there a risk these words are still affecting the decisions you make today?

Then think about people you were inspired by when you were young. What is it about them you found most motivating? How did they get to where they are now? Read biographies and talk to people in your organisation who have invested in their growth.

I know this feels like I'm putting thumbscrews on you but you're not the woman carrying water from the well 20 kilometres away. When we compare our white privilege in the western world with that of women in developing nations, we sometimes feel that self-development is a massive luxury. Yet we have the benefit of being able to pursue our learning goals. We need to act. We have a choice.

If you're reluctant to enrol in new learning because you have to juggle so many commitments, consider who can take some of those commitments off your hands.

Is it possible for you to ask someone else to feed the children one night per week? Can your best friend pick them up from school and take them to netball training so that you can study?

Some women feel stuck because they can't see a support structure to fall back on. Some have not been taught how to ask for help. Others are stubborn or ashamed and feel they have to do everything on their own. There is no disgrace in phoning a friend, your parents, or a trusted neighbour. And if you have a partner, he's a parent too—not a babysitter. At the end of this chapter, I encourage you to talk about your aspirations with your family and friends. This will help them to help you.

Continue to challenge yourself. Are the barriers in your mind and those you hear from others true? Yours could be the loudest voice of protest.

Stop mauling your mojo

There's a memorable scene in the 1989 movie, *When Harry Met Sally*, where Sally and Harry are sitting in a café eating a sandwich. Harry tells Sally that when he beds a woman, she has an 'okay' time. Sally asks how he can be so sure. She tells a surprised Harry that most women, at some time in their lives, fake orgasm. He won't believe her, so Sally fakes an orgasm right there, in the café, to prove her point. Another woman looks to the waiter and says, 'I'll have what she's having'. (If you have never seen the movie, it is worth viewing the 3-minute clip on *YouTube*—hilarious.)

It is easy to assume someone else is having a better life than you: they have more opportunities, less stress, and so on. Assumptions like these stop you from living your best life. In reality, you don't know the whole picture, and it's irrelevant to the choices you make anyway.

Envy reduces energy. It mauls your mojo. When women get stuck in this way of thinking, it holds them back. It's not a productive or healthy use of your time to feel inferior, disappointed in yourself or devalued. Comparison is the thief of joy.

Comparisons are easy to make, yet they seldom serve women. When women compare their lives negatively to others, it is counter-productive. Leon Festinger developed social comparison theory in 1954. I wrote about this in my book, *Cutting through the grass ceiling*. Festinger's theory explains the comparisons we make between ourselves and others. When we compare adversely, we seek illusory perfection. Sometimes, we turn our friends and colleagues into rivals. We are threatened by them getting to the spoils before us as if there's not enough to go around. This destructive thinking can influence our behaviours and decisions.

Some friends have more significant opportunities, more financial security, and broader networks. Does that stop you from doing things to improve your life? Your friends can't do this for you but they can be your biggest champions and provide insights into how they achieved their successes.

The flipside is a favourable comparison, which can be motivating and help you achieve your aims.

 Exercise 2

Choose one friend or colleague you envy and to whom you compare yourself. Next, draw a table with two columns. In the first column, note down the comparisons one by one. In the second column, write one thing to do for each of those comparisons to help you progress with your development.

For example, in column one, you may write, 'I envy the way Melissa influences decisions at meetings. I'd like to get my points across the way she does'. In this instance, column two might read, 'I will find appropriate training in negotiation and influencing skills, and I'll listen to the words Melissa uses to see if there's something I can learn'.

> When you have completed this, add one more column. Imagine your comparison person was making a list of their own by comparing themselves to you. What positives about your life and career would they notice with possible envy? You might be surprised that for every woman to whom you compare yourself, there is another who compares herself to you and who thinks you have all the luck.

Maximise your mojo by committing to be the inspiration for other women—you are worthy of being inspirational.

It's not just the job

Dr Jenny Brockis is an author, speaker and lifestyle medicine physician in Perth, Western Australia. She is passionate about people, performance and practical solutions to improving cognitive health and wellbeing.

Jenny writes in detail about her experience with burnout, denying her needs and putting everybody else first (including her patients). I was fortunate to have Jenny as a guest on my *Afternoon with an author* webcast.

In the interview, Jenny spoke about her book, *Thriving mind*. In it, she reveals the three keys to thriving: mindfulness, making a deliberate choice to be well and seeking help with connection. (I will cover more about the importance of connection in a later chapter.) These three keys help people tackle the demands of modern life, including the weights of the workplace.

Thriving is about all of your life and how you contribute to society. I know from my clients' and my own experiences that putting yourself first is more significant than prioritising your work.

I know it is hard to consider yourself first on your list of people for whom you care. It takes time to unlearn the habits of a lifetime—until now. There is yet another excellent reason for you to do so. It's better for everyone you love. If you don't accept this idea for yourself, do it to be a better partner, parent, daughter, friend, or colleague. See, it's not selfish after all.

You may have fears about how your family and friends will react to this 'new' you, the woman who has stopped saying yes to every request and no longer prioritises them every time. How are they going to judge you? Will they still love you? These questions can churn your stomach and keep you awake at night.

I have armed you with evidence about the benefits of self-care and why it matters. You know you will be a better person when you are higher on your list of concerns.

There are always exceptions. There will be times in life when there is pressure to do everything at once (like writing a book, and running a business and a household— argh!) I accept there are times when balance means your development will be secondary to other needs. My point, however, is this can't be a lifelong state.

Be brave and have a conversation with your family. See what they have noticed in you when you are at your happiest and flourishing. Ask them what they see right now? Is there a difference? What advice would they give you?

One strategy I offer my coaching clients is a self-awareness 360-degree tool. Clients select ten people from a diverse base to interview, including people they know well such as an intimate partner, to people who might know them at work and are less familiar. My clients then interview the ten people by asking five questions to which they must listen to the responses and only say 'thank you' at the end. There is no interjecting or asking for further information.

The tool is helpful in understanding another person's experience of you; it is their truth and doesn't have to become yours.

Feedback helps you understand your impact on others and reveals what they notice about your happiness or other states. It's often a revelation for the women I coach.

Your self-talk could be the most significant barrier you face at present. It's time to challenge your wistful language and connect to the worthy words you wrote initially.

Let's wrap this up

You've learned why it's important to develop yourself throughout your life, and it's not luxuriant or selfish. You've read how lifelong learning helps those people you care about as much as you. Investing in yourself is more significant than your job—it makes you a better citizen.

I have outlined some obstacles to overcome, such as:

- The expectations others may have of you.
- The beliefs you hold about yourself.
- The comparisons you make between yourself and others.
- Your self-talk.

I hope you will evaluate where you sit on the wistful versus worthy language continuum. I encourage you to talk with your family about how important your future development is for you. Tell them you're reading this book and why.

I'll leave you with this note from Adam Grant, an organisational psychologist at Wharton, bestselling author of *Originals* and *Think again*, and host of the TED podcast *WorkLife*. Grant is one of my favourite writers of the decade. Grant's comments apply to all of us, not just those starting their careers:

'Your first job doesn't have to make the world a better place—it just needs to make you better. It isn't selfish to invest in your development. You do that when you go to college, and it applies to your early career too. Learning today prepares you for more impact tomorrow.'

Coming up in Chapter Two, I'll tell you why you must not delay your development and I'll outline the costs of putting your growth on hold.

CHAPTER TWO

Why you can't wait

According to academics at the Kellogg School of Management, Northwestern University, Illinois, progress in a person's career doesn't happen by magic. People have to plan. The article, *Take 5: How to take charge of your professional development,* by Anne Ford, outlines five steps to successful career planning:

1. Building influence.
2. Learning to negotiate.
3. Mentoring other people.
4. **Continue learning, even when you reach your career high point.**
5. **Self-reflection.**

I have highlighted these last two points, as they are critical to success.

My wish for all women is to fall in love with their work and to not delay their development. Women need to keep growing to maximise expertise, opportunities, happiness, and health. When they don't, they risk falling behind and becoming deskilled.

I agree with Jamila Rizvi (author, presenter and political commentator) who says women's self-worth is entwined in their careers and reputations. In her book, *Not just lucky,* Rizvi says,

'The professional is the personal, so women feel strongly about it'.

Yet women often wait for employers to offer them learning opportunities. Time is too important for women to waste. Women need to get busy learning or get busy languishing. Don't miss chances.

No one else can learn for you, and growth opportunities won't always land at your feet. It would be best if you took control of your career and your growth.

When women ask for support and use formal organisational processes to best effect, they identify aspirations and make the most of their options.

Pay your way

Joh is a former coaching client whom I interviewed for this book. I have always admired Joh's commitment to her learning and growth. Because she has worked in small non-profit agencies with low budgets, Joh has never waited for her employers to offer her training. She researches to find courses to meet her needs. Joh also funds all of her development programs—including her coaching sessions with me.

Joh sought out coaching because she was very clear about what she wanted to achieve and she was ready to act. On reflection, she thought it might have been to do with her maturity and experience (as younger women often ignore the urge for action).

We talked about the different life stages of learning. Joh recalled the training she attended in her twenties where she was encouraged to spend ten per cent of her income on self-education, annually. She described it as ensuring she sharpens every tool in the toolbox.

Joh couldn't remember a time in her career when she didn't have a mentor or coach in some form. Her view is that women need quality mentoring throughout life.

Unlike Joh, many women wait to be asked before they take on any learning program. They hesitate to take control of their growth and development.

Self-help books and personality quizzes in glossy magazines don't give these women what they need, and this is why women have to take charge to improve their career options.

Some women are reluctant to negotiate access to funds for training. They fear damaging authoritative relationships at work. Even when a company spruiks its 'employer of choice' status, its employees can still find it hard to ask for what they need for advancement. Women like Joh put their money where their mouth is and back themselves. Others don't believe they have the financial resources or support from their family to do so.

If this is you, think again. You might be surprised that what you'd like to do isn't as expensive as you believe or may not take as much time as you thought. When you don't know what's required, you give up your power. Become informed and in control.

> **Exercise 3**
>
> I invite you to be curious: check what's on offer at your workplace. Search in the community and look at adult learning programs, workshops, and seminars. There are opportunities to learn new skills without committing to a significant expense.

A scarcity mindset will create doubt in your capacity to invest in yourself. While you may have real concerns about available cash or time, this is not insurmountable. Workplace programs, sponsorships, scholarships, and fee help from the government are all options. Save for your aspirations and talk to your accountant about the self-education expenses to claim at tax time.

It's never too late to invest

I once worked with a man who went back to university at 65 to complete a PhD. I was 25 at the time and was astounded by his commitment to learning. Now, at 55, I understand it.

My former client Kerry, whom I interviewed for this book, recalled the difficulties she faced in her work. She was at the final stage of her career, and:

'… there was a lot of change occurring in the sector. And although change can be good, it didn't feel like a coordinated change. My role was quite isolated with very few people I could confide in—where I could open myself up. So mentoring was where I headed'.

Kerry fluctuated between wanting to retire or hold on to her job. An interesting thing occurred about midway through our mentoring engagement. To her surprise, Kerry found that the learning and reflection she had done led her in a new career direction. She set a time frame for leaving her job, which met her own and her employer's needs. Then she returned to study to develop skills for a new occupation. Kerry was in her sixties.

Kerry said that without mentoring:

'… I think I'd probably still be sitting in the same role and becoming increasingly disenchanted with myself. And I've realised that's not the way to be. I've got control over certain things and influence over certain things. And the biggest one is me'.

You might believe it's counterintuitive to jump into new learning later in your working life. Like most things, there's never a best time—except for the present. Remember the Nike advertisement? **Just do it.** Start reaping the benefits of learning, no matter your age.

Some women, like me, commit to multiple development programs at once (phew!). I have found it essential to maintain a balance, not just financially but also in energy and time. Options include deferring an enrolment to study later, spreading a shorter program over a more extended period, or taking up a payment plan. There are many ways to make learning possible across your life.

Like the Kellogg Northwestern article's advice and Joh's case study, I'd like you to consider a **professional development investment plan**. Think of your plan like a wardrobe stylist. Let's say you spend $2,500 on clothes per year only to leave the tags on half of them and send them, unworn, to the opportunity shop the following year. A wardrobe consultant or image stylist is the expert to help you find clothes to suit you and bring you joy. They don't worry about how old you are. You invest in their help and buy clothes you wear every week. This gives you value and power. So does your professional development investment plan. When you focus on value instead of cost, more choices seem possible.

Here are my tips:

- Decide to invest a percentage of your annual income in your development every year.
- Clear space in your life and make time for development. What can you let go of now?
- Find out what is available to you in your workplace such as mentoring and coaching programs, study leave, and internal training courses.
- Determine the commitment required to complete your desired activity.
- Develop an immediate, 12-month and 3-year plan.

Nobody can do it for you

'Sascha' placed her development on hold for many years through several jobs and the birth of her two children. When she relocated with her family, Sascha took up a new job. At this time, she noticed how her self-belief had slipped. Sascha wanted to thrive in her new role and to advance further.

Sascha approached her employer about leadership coaching. She was supported and encouraged, but the business owners said they did not have the resources to commit to the fee. Sascha decided to pay for her coaching and signed up to a six-month program.

After the program, Sascha's husband told her he noticed she was using new language to describe herself. Sascha is more confident and happy and she enjoys her work. She says she is taking responsibility for things whereas a year ago she wouldn't have. Her employers are delegating significant projects, and she's been offered an ongoing contract.

Sascha's decision to go it alone was worthwhile. She waited long enough and took control of her development.

Nobody else is going to do your development for you. If you want to be independent of your employer and not reliant on what they offer you, take charge. You can't always rely on your sponsoring managers to make things happen for you. They are busy and they're not mind-readers. They might not have a budget large enough to help you succeed but this doesn't mean they don't want you to be successful.

Could you be cutting off your nose to spite your face by paying for your development? It is a factor to consider. Maybe you are blowing your own money when you could be negotiating for an employer contribution.

Like Joh, Kerry, and Sascha, I know that an investment in yourself gives you a bonus: you pay for the things you want to do, and you dictate the terms. You get to double-dip *and* accept the programs your employer provides. There are exceptions though. If a specific skill or qualification is mandatory in your job, your employer can call the shots and hold you accountable to undertake training. For everything else, you have a choice.

> **Exercise 4**
>
> Think about what you require in the year ahead to do your work. What development is obligatory for you to complete for your employer, and what can you choose for yourself? Please reflect. It will help you with the next theme.

Use the formal processes to best effect

At her annual review, Nic identified leadership training as a goal. The following year, her manager asked her to apply for an internal leadership program. Nic was uncertain about whether she was the right fit and almost declined the offer. With her manager's encouragement and a phone call to the person running the program (me), she decided to join. Nic leapt, and she loved it.

'Hayley' also used her performance review to gain organisational investment for her needs. Hayley's review fell straight after her promotion, and she told her executive she had specific challenges to address. They granted her funds for a new manager's program, which didn't proceed due to the COVID-19 pandemic. Hayley didn't want to waste her budget allocation or see it disappear. She asked that the funds be diverted into a coaching program to support her leadership learning needs.

The annual performance review process helps women identify aspirations. Employers invest a percentage of their payroll in learning and development for their staff. Use it or lose it. The funds are not cumulative.

Most employees and employers don't maximise the performance review process. Yet the process can provide a practical way to alert your manager to the development you want to undertake.

Should you put your hand up for development or not? What if a program isn't the right fit for now? Think about Nic's example: she didn't assume and took steps to find out more.

Some women think it's demanding or presumptuous to ask for support from the organisation, especially in a performance review. Take it from me (as a former CEO and general manager), there's frustration in handing back unexpended learning and development funds each budget year only to suffer cutbacks because people aren't using the funds. I also guarantee men will ask—you should too.

You might work for a firm where learning and development aren't valued, where there's no formal review process or system. Bummer. Consider the courses you can pay for yourself and whether you wish to stay with a company that won't invest in its people, even when it can afford to. You might have limited parameters in which to play, and this might deflate your hopes. Don't be disheartened. Take control of the things that are controllable.

For the rest of you, dust off your last two annual reviews. Did you action all the learning you said you would? Is anything not complete, and is it still relevant? Your findings form the first part of your professional development investment plan.

Check the annual learning calendar in your workplace. Talk to the human resources or learning and development coordinator and explore what's on offer.

Let's wrap this up

Many women delay their professional and personal growth, and I hope you now understand why it's crucial to invest in yourself. I've told you stories about women who control their professional development and are not dependent on their employers. I have shown you how to maximise what's on offer in your workplace.

CHAPTER TWO: WHY YOU CAN'T WAIT

I know I've given you lots to think about in this chapter and a long list of homework. My message is this: stay curious, become aware of what's available, and invest a percentage of your annual income in your learning every year.

Given I have encouraged you to spend your hard-earned cash on developing your career, next, I'll cover why making money matters.

CHAPTER THREE

Making money matters

'Debbie' was a mid-level manager in a non-profit agency. After several years, Debbie's job was made redundant, and she was offered a termination package as part of her contract. Debbie's partner had not been in paid work for a decade and was the primary carer for their sons. Debbie's job had been the family's security. Now, it was gone. Except for two things.

Debbie had kept up her contributions to the family's investments throughout her employment and had financed her development to stay current in her industry. As a result, Debbie found a new job within three months. Financial stability allowed Debbie to take a job of her choice in order to have less responsibility than her former position. She opted for less stress, a shorter commute, one work-from-home day per week, and more time with her boys.

Because of their investments, Debbie and her wife knew they could keep their lifestyle for two years without either partner working. Having this security meant they could make different decisions. Debbie knew she had time to recover from redundancy, ease into her new workplace, and consider her next steps later.

In her book, *Blind spots*, Bec Brideson referenced an Ernst & Young study which showed that by 2028 women will control close to 75 per cent of discretionary spending worldwide. But it seems they still mostly spend on themselves last.

Unlike Debbie, women often have fewer funds for their development because they put their own needs last. These decisions compound in the same way interest on a loan does. Many women don't bother to get advice about money.

They figure they will catch up on what they need to know later. I have met women who say, 'I'll invest later when I have more money to spare'. There's *never* more money to spare. Most people live to their income level. Women need to be more deliberate about their savings.

Some women work to support a household income, not for their personal objectives. They may rely on others, such as their employer or spouse, for any study or courses they wish to take. The risk here is that they forgo or delay learning opportunities.

Women can have a life with latitude when they plan and invest in their professional and personal growth. Having a **financial plan** gives women the capacity to spend money on their development throughout their career.

The more women invest in learning, the better chance they have of making more money in higher paid jobs. More income leads to contributing more to their retirement funds and reducing their dependency upon others. Less money can lead to a lower standard of living in old age. If the Australian Royal Commission into Aged Care Quality and Safety has taught us anything, it is making money matters—for all of us.

Girls need financial role models too. One of Debbie's aspirations was to model to her sons the importance of preparing for a secure future. Women can set a strong example for children by talking about how they invest in themselves for now and for later.

We need to understand the relationship between money and self, where the association comes from, and how wistful versus worthy self-talk affects financial decisions.

Go for growth

If you are an Australian reader, you'll have heard of superannuation. For readers outside Australia, superannuation or 'super' is compulsory for all people who work and reside here. A legislated percentage of an individual's salary is directly invested by their employer. Workers also have an option to make further personal contributions to their fund. A person's superannuation balance provides an income when they retire. It's the equivalent of a pension fund, for example, in the United Kingdom.

Starting in 2009 until 2014, the 'from little things, big things grow' superannuation campaign ran on behalf of industry funds. The campaign used Australian music artist and songwriter Paul Kelly's song to encourage people to invest in their future. The campaign was aimed at all working Australians, helping us to understand the need for financial security when we conclude paid work.

I'm 55, and I recall the introduction of superannuation for all people in the workforce. Saving for the future was not embedded in our national DNA. Past generations of men, whose wives had not been in paid work, retired with an aged pension supplied by the federal government, funded through taxation revenue. For many households, it was an adequate income at the time. People lived shorter lives, and let's face it, most older people had more modest lifestyles.

Times have changed. The vast majority of us need to plan well for retirement, a longer life and more adventure. Women can't depend on men for their financial futures anymore—women know better now.

Women aren't insulting their partners when they work towards their own financial goals. They don't need to feel guilty about earning capacity or investment. Their financial security is as important to them as their families.

When women back themselves and invest in their learning and development, it creates options for the remainder of their lives.

Have you ever felt guilty about not contributing as much to the household budget as you think you should? Have you ever felt wistful about the things you couldn't afford to do? They're awful feelings. They undermine your confidence.

You might have grown up with traditional expectations and roles. Your role models (parents, grandparents, and extended family) may have managed their finances in ways that impact your decisions today. For instance, if your parents didn't spend money on education, you might not either. Or if your mother put her own goals last, you might feel self-indulgent spending money on your personal advancement.

It is important to reflect on how you think about money. You're worthy of having options and future security. It's not an indulgence.

There are times when investing is harder. You may be experiencing financial stress, like Debbie's redundancy, or you may have been away from the workforce, for instance, on parental leave. I am not a financial adviser, and I am not offering financial advice. There are, however, many resources to help you understand money and how to save it. Examples are Melissa Browne's *More money for shoes*, Susie Orman's *Women & money* and Scott Pape's *The barefoot investor*. Most superannuation funds also have financial planners who will answer any questions.

Have a conversation with your partner. Include the kids in a family meeting if they are old enough. Talk about what matters to each of you and how you would like to create space for those things. Talk about your learning and development needs and why you want to invest in yourself.

Personal growth and financial security is your responsibility, as much as your partner's. Please don't leave it to him or her. Make sure you have a financial plan of your own.

Be a development role model

I have never met a mother who doesn't want to be a role model for her children. While conversations about modelling often include education, they don't always include money. Securing children's futures starts by setting an example for them. Children are our legacy.

When women take care of the money stuff, kids have a better chance of doing so in their own lives. So do grandchildren. Women who believe they are worthy go on to create generations who invest in learning and growth.

Louisa's story shows how women invest in other people, often without thinking, while not prioritising the investment in themselves. Louisa shared a metaphor: imagine attending a family wedding interstate. She might pay for flights, accommodation, and new outfits for herself and her husband. It wouldn't only be a dress; she would buy shoes, a bag and earrings. Then there would be new clothes for the kids. Louisa said many women would consider it reasonable to spend substantial money on a family wedding but would question whether to invest $5,000 or $6,000 for their professional support.

When I interviewed Louisa, she talked about the importance of investing in mentoring support, which is as important, if not more, as spending your earnings on a family event. The $5,500 she spent on mentoring gave her a more substantial return than any wedding outfit. Not comparing apples with apples here, but I understand Louisa's analogy.

Some women pride themselves on placing their children's learning needs first. When they are small, it may feel like there is no other choice. But is this realistic? And is it what you and your children want to remember?

Continue your family conversations about goals and aspirations. Talk about what you're studying, the workshops or conferences you attend, the things you're looking forward to learning and how you're going to pay for them.

Help your children become familiar with investing in themselves and their learning by having these discussions at the dinner table.

There will be influences from other families you know and your own family that will pull you in another direction. There may be criticism. Be ready to counter it with examples and positive stories from television, social media, and women's networks. Please talk about the possibilities you are creating and why you are proud of your goals. Don't shy away. Focus on the people who lift you and are proud of your drive.

Understand your money biases

In 2008, the Australian Government's Financial Literacy Foundation produced a report called *Financial literacy: Women understanding money*. More than a decade ago, the report found Australian women had more choices about money management than at any other time in history. Women had access to credit, mobile banking, and investment options. The report showed women were frequently the decision-makers about day-to-day household spending and were involved in decisions about their financial future. Despite this, there was evidence of women's lower average incomes, time away from the workforce for family reasons, lower resulting superannuation and the imperative for women's savings to stretch further because of their longer average lifespan.

It is essential to understand what causes biases towards money. How does wistful self-talk affect decisions about investing in learning and personal development? When women know where their beliefs and values come from, they can make informed choices.

Have you ever criticised yourself for 'wasting' money? Or described your spending as 'frivolous' or 'spendthrift'? Do you look at money from a perspective of scarcity or abundance? Beliefs about money affect the choices women make—as the Financial Literacy report showed. Knowing what this means for you gives you financial power.

Test your biases about money by reading the article from AMP on their website called *How our subconscious affects our attitude towards money*. The article describes the six cognitive biases influencing how we spend and save.

You might be afraid to understand your attitudes to money. Changing habits can be scary. You might feel you have to give up too much freedom or you may be fearful that others will judge you for investing in yourself. Such views are deep-seated. It takes time and education to shift beliefs. Don't just do it for you. Do it for your children or philanthropic reasons.

Some of you will be pushing back, feeling the world is too materialistic anyway. You might be over conversations about money and seeking a simpler life. The truth is, no matter how much wealth you wish to create, nobody except you will invest in your future.

Let's wrap this up

Women can have a life with latitude when they plan for their development and set aside funds to realise their plans. The more serious women are about learning, the better opportunities present themselves and the more money they can earn.

More money means a healthier, happier, fulfilled old age and some neat stuff along the way before they reach that time.

Traditional expectations about money and family and friends' influences help create our biases towards money—how we earn it and how we invest it. Women are sometimes reluctant and fearful about investing in themselves for fear of being seen as selfish, wasteful, and neglectful of other priorities.

Develop a family and personal financial plan to help you achieve your goals. Take time to understand your biases about money and how best to make what you earn work better for you.

Speaking of investing in development, in the next chapter, I'll show you why your growth doesn't have to be dependent upon high-cost university degrees and how to enrich your learning in other ways.

CHAPTER FOUR

Don't I need another degree?

When women talk to me about career advancement and contentment, it's not long before they raise the idea of further education. Most already have a degree, even two. These women ask: If I want to get a promotion or shift careers, do I need another technical degree? Or, if I want to get into leadership, must I do a Master of Business Administration (MBA)? Many people have already told them that additional study is essential.

I want to clarify three points.

1. University is only one option. You *don't* have to return to university (or to ever have been) to study for your career of choice.

2. Success requires more than technical skill; you need soft skills such as self-knowledge and emotional intelligence. Expand your thinking about the skills you need.

3. Do not start a degree to please somebody else. If you're studying, make sure you are doing so to please you.

In short, university qualifications are helpful but they are not the only way to learn.

We are going to talk about the alternatives (and the risks). For example, you might overcommit your time and money, and increase your stress levels by taking on a degree when you don't have passion for the subject matter. Plus, it won't get you where you want to go.

I'll share stories from people I've helped within my practice who have found other ways to succeed. I'll refer to various leadership programs and the outcomes for their graduates. I'll explore the future of work and the skills, attributes and support we all need to enable long and fulfilling careers.

I am not anti-university. I have three degrees. (What was I thinking?) Degrees are delightful when you're clear about why you need one and when study excites you. More about this later.

Development is more than a degree

In 2019, I ran a survey on the platform LinkedIn. I asked people about their mentoring and coaching experiences and whether those experiences benefited their careers and justified their investment. Over 50 people commented within 24 hours of the post going live. Without exception, respondents shared their views that having a professional coach or mentor had been the most valuable investment they had made in their leadership careers.

Let's look at an example from 'Lindy'. Within six months of starting her coaching program, Lindy added around $30,000 to her annual income. Tell me where you have found a degree with such a guarantee—I'll share the news with ALL my clients.

When Lindy first came to me, she was perplexed. Should she invest $10,000 per year for several years and do a second master's degree? Or should she spend the equivalent of one year's study on a 12-month coaching program?

Lindy's goal was to prepare for recruitment to a senior public service role. Lindy knew she needed to develop her leadership skills to win those roles. When Lindy weighed up her options, a degree didn't cut it. Yes, it would provide more in-depth academic knowledge and the feel-good factor, but it wouldn't fast-track her into the leadership role she so desired. (It would have taken her six years.) Lindy decided to invest her funds in a coaching program with me. What resulted was a promotion within the first six months.

Many women have a bias that tertiary education is better than all other options. Such a bias prevents them from seeing different development opportunities. Naturally, it's a widespread misunderstanding. It blocks your ability to see what else is available. The blinkers were off for Lindy.

So, what are the alternatives? Coaching is but one way. Andrea Hogg coordinates the Australian Rural Leadership Program. It is the premier leadership program for regional leaders through the Australian Rural Leadership Foundation. The program has an annual intake of about 25 and includes a trip overseas to study leadership and a week-long camping adventure. 'Participants in the program have often applied multiple times before acceptance,' Andrea says. The program's popularity and high subscription level show the importance leaders place on experiential training outside a tertiary environment.

It can be challenging to discern the best uses of your time and budget. Not every leadership program has solid branding like universities. As Regional Leadership Australia says in its mission statement, so many people *search endlessly, fruitlessly and frustratingly for the tools, templates and connections they need.*

I graduated from the Gippsland Community Leadership Program in 2001. I called it my 'Clayton's MBA'. Those old enough to remember the non-alcoholic beverage, 'Claytons', will know what I mean. The drink was marketed towards drinkers who wanted to enjoy a 'spirit', guilt-free. Claytons became a colloquialism for a viable alternative.

But despite its humble profile, the program was a catalyst for me to change my direction and step into my first CEO role. The Gippsland Community Leadership Program formed the basis of my future career.

If leadership programs interest you but you're confused about choosing one, head to the end of this chapter where you will find *10 questions to consider before applying for a leadership program*.

Perhaps you know or work with people who have several degrees and are thriving. Excellent. What I'd like you to do is also be curious about how much their degrees have compounded their earning capacity and their contentment. What was the total return on their investment? Ask them to talk with you over a coffee before you make a decision.

Why is somebody with three university qualifications suggesting you don't need one? Fair point. Tertiary study doesn't equip you for work but it does give you a curious mind. The real learning starts after completing the course.

I want you to consider a range of opinions before deciding on returning to study or starting in the first place. There are exceptions. Some professions have mandatory qualifications. For example, if you aim to be a clinical psychologist, the professional body, the Australian Psychological Society, will say you can't enter the field without the required degree and supervision. If you want to become an academic and teach at university, you will need a PhD.

This is why you need to prepare your professional development investment plan. Do your career goals require a mandatory qualification? If yes, take the time to interview people who have your desired job already. Ask if they got their degree before they started the job. You might be surprised at how often 'mandatory' translates to 'desirable'.

Although it can feel a bit intrusive to ask people how they got into their roles, you'd be surprised at how generous people are with information.

Some professional biases still exist about people who don't have degrees. These are deeply embedded. So much so, the Victorian Government announced a policy in November 2020 to scrap the state's different school completion schemes. The stigma reported by students undertaking the Year 12 Victorian Certificate of Applied Learning compared with those in the Victorian Certificate of Education was a stimulus for change.

Successful careers are more than technical

There are specific skills and attributes that enable us to have long and fulfilling working lives. It's prudent to focus our attention on the emerging trends for development such as soft skills. Authors like Brené Brown, Angela Duckworth and Daniel Goleman write about vulnerability, grit, and emotional intelligence as being more important than technical skills. It's helpful to understand the future of work and contemporary thinking about skills development. This knowledge helps us to plan growth opportunities.

You could be thinking, *that's all fine if you're born with those traits* or *it's nature, not nurture—those skills cannot be learned.* You may also believe learning is exclusive to study, not personal reflection and self-analysis.

Self-knowledge and academic intelligence are not mutually exclusive or dependent. Bill Gates dropped out of Harvard University. Yet the American business magnate and co-founder of Microsoft is one of the world's wealthiest people. Gates credits some of his success to his commitment to coaching. He gave a TED Talk in 2013 with Eric Schmidt called *Everyone needs a coach.*

Technical skills are essential for some jobs. For example, real estate agents, financial advisers and insurance brokers all require specific certifications. **Technical skill requirements often change. People skills will remain critical forever.**

When you look at your Worthy v Wistful Words chart, is there anything on the wistful side about your personal development? Something you wish you had done? The professional mentor you never engaged? If you're sorry you haven't put your hand up for a personal development program, add it to your plan. Find out what you need to commit to in order to complete it.

Your most significant barrier right now might be to challenge your own bias about learning. Suppose you believe knowledge is purely for technical or academic purposes. In that case, I invite you to contest your thinking and consider how your personal development could take you further in your career.

Don't study to please somebody else

All her working life, 'Jade' told herself she wouldn't land an executive role without an MBA. The MBA hung over her like a phantom. Jade told me MBAs had become more common, and she assumed that they were critical for leadership roles. Jade discovered, to her delight, that she was wrong.

With her strong background and experience, and her existing Bachelor's degree, she scored a senior executive role in a large organisation supervising more than 250 staff. Jade is so engrossed in her job that she has neither the time nor the inclination to go back to study.

If you are like Jade, I advise you to order Alicia McKay's book, *You don't need an MBA: Leadership lessons that cut through the crap*. McKay is New Zealand's straight-talking strategist and has worked with some of the most senior leaders in Australia and across the pond.

CHAPTER FOUR: DON'T I NEED ANOTHER DEGREE?

Degrees are delightful when you know where you are aiming. If you're planning to pursue extra tertiary study, know your 'why'. Don't do a degree because somebody else said you should. You will regret it if you find it's not the right choice. Once you have committed for you, your family, and your employer, be sure it's what you want.

Tiana has compelling reasons for her PhD candidacy. Her doctorate is important to her. It represents her powerful commitment to her community, her nation, and her long-term goals. Her world-first research excites and inspires her. She has the potential to change how health services are provided in regional and rural communities. Tiana is crystal clear on her reasons for study. Coaching helped her find this clarity, which will ensure her commitment through the tough times when she wavers.

By now, you'll be reflecting on all the advice you've had from people you respect. They've told you to get another degree to pursue your career goals. Don't ignore the advice; they are viewpoints for you to consider. Add them to the guidance bank you're gathering, along with the information in this chapter.

The counter-argument here is that no learning is wasted. One of my former clients, Leah, started a bookkeeping course to help her with her family's business finances. She disliked it but finished it anyway. While managing some competing priorities, she deferred several subjects but went back to finish the last units, knowing it would be helpful to have the skills. Does she wish she had used those funds for another form of development? Yes, sometimes. In the end, she knows the course will enhance the way she manages the books.

We get one crack at life. I urge you to make the choices to fulfil and stretch you the most.

How's your self-talk at this point? Is your desire to go back to study coming from the right place? Make sure it's not driven by negativity or a deep belief that you're not enough as you are. If doing another degree is part of your worthy words language, go for it. If it's not, think about who you are trying to please.

Let's wrap this up

You have learned that you don't need to have another degree to extend yourself. University is one learning option. There are skills beyond the technical that stand us in good stead for the future. Tertiary education isn't required to learn these skills. Study is remarkable when we are excited and inspired by it, and when we are headed towards our orienting point.

Without a degree, you may encounter professional biases. You might also need to challenge your preconceptions about learning. Check your inner voice. It could be driving your decisions about tertiary education.

At this point, I hope you will:

- Take the time to prepare your development plan, including a budget.
- Research your dream jobs and the mandatory qualifications you need.
- Talk with people about whether those qualifications are compulsory.

In the next chapter, I'll discuss ambition and our attitudes to it. It's a follow-on from our examination of skills and academic development, and what drives us to desire these things.

By the way, Jade says she might like to do an MBA one day to say she's done it. $50,000–$100,000 for intellectual stimulation is one heck of a commitment. Good on you, Jade.

10 questions to consider before applying for a leadership program

1. What are my primary aspirations?

   All leadership programs have application processes. It's helpful to think about what you want to achieve by undertaking a program. This will assist you in choosing the best program for your needs. It will also mean you have thought about some potential answers to application and interview questions in advance. Here are a few examples:

   - I'm seeking to develop my leadership skills.
   - I'm hoping to understand more about leadership theory.
   - I'm looking to lead in a regional community, including as a volunteer.
   - I want to increase my visibility in my industry.
   - I'm seeking new and broader networks than I already have.

2. Do I know someone who has completed a leadership program?

   It's likely you know someone, for example, in your workplace who has completed a program. Have a conversation about their experiences, what they enjoyed most, and what they wished was different. This will help you gain clarity about your aspirations.

3. What are the top three things I will gain from undertaking a leadership program?

   To understand if it's the right time for you to apply, think about what you'd like to gain.

4. What three things will I bring to a program?

   Leadership programs are a two-way street. It's not all about the benefit to you. What can you give back to the broader group so others can benefit from your participation?

5. What are my employer's and my budgets?

   Leadership programs can range from $5,000 to upwards of $15,000. There are various payment plans and fee concessions along with scholarships for some programs. It's important to know what you can spend and whether you will be applying for scholarship assistance.

6. Do I have a preference for a non-profit or a commercial program?

   Non-profit groups and for-profit companies run programs. You might have a preference for the program you attend, and it's good to think about this before you apply.

7. How far can I travel?

   Do you see yourself travelling long distances to complete the program? Or would you prefer something closer to home?

8. How much time can I commit to a program?

   Are you looking for a short-term program, for example, a one-week residential, or are you seeking to spend a year plus in a program? What will be the impacts of short- and long-term programs on your family and work?

9. Who might be able to act as a referee?

   Most leadership programs will require you to provide two or more referees. When you choose someone to act in this capacity, organise to have a conversation with them about your aspirations. It's good to ask them what would be the one piece of advice they would give you right now about your leadership development.

10. Does my employer / volunteer organisation have a list of leadership programs they prefer or recommend?

    Some organisations prefer specific leadership programs, and it's best to know this before applying elsewhere. It's also good to know if there's a list that could help you decide on the best program for your needs.

CHAPTER FIVE

But ambition isn't nice

Former US First Lady, Michelle Obama, in her book, *Becoming,* writes:

'I can admit now that I was driven not just by logic, but by some reflexive wish for other people's approval too'.

I have never met Michelle Obama. If I were granted a wish by a genie to have dinner with three famous women of my choosing, Michelle would be on my list. She seems nice. She strikes me as ambitious for her husband and children, and for herself. Her description of her need to please others, and meet their expectations, is potent.

When my clients talk to me about ambition, invariably, there is an uncomfortable point. They associate ambition with putting their needs first. Many people describe ambitious women as bitchy, ballsy, and intimidating. The word 'ambition' brings out our most profound biases, conscious or otherwise. Likewise, many people associate the word 'nice' with weakness. Being pleasant is seen as unassertive and girlish. It seems we have replaced the term nice with 'kind'. Nice has become taboo: it's not to be spoken, unless in criticism or to describe food.

This chapter will reframe how to think about these terms and show how women can lead with both characteristics. Nice women do get the corner office. And there is a growing number of them in leadership positions around the world.

Myth-busting

Remember my niece's question? She wanted to know what being worthy meant to me. A precise moment of worthiness for me was discovering the work of Brené Brown. Brown is an American researcher whose work confirms that ambition is not a shameful thing nor is vulnerability. Leading with vulnerability seems to be what I have done throughout my years of managing other people. Being ambitious and nice at the same time is possible.

Women need to know how to bust the myths about ambition and character. The *Cambridge Dictionary* defines myth-busting as showing something usually thought to be true is not accurate or is different from the usual description. I plan to work with the Cambridge definition in this chapter.

For as long as I recall, women have received glacial drifts of advice about ambition. It is time to melt the ice and unfreeze this advice. Women need to know what information to heed for the best impact on their future thoughts. When women don't have this discretion, they risk feeling stalled.

Women who seek coaching with me describe feeling like dormant plants just waiting for the drought to break. Worthy thoughts about niceness and ambition give women the drought-busting rain they crave.

Ambition is the new attractive, and ambitious women draw others to them. When women change their self-talk from wistful to worthy, they move beyond the people-pleasing phase (as shown in Chapter One).

CHAPTER FIVE: BUT AMBITION ISN'T NICE

Nice isn't negative

One of the nicest people I know is a woman I respect and admire for her ability to draw boundaries. She is not afraid to say no to requests. She keeps her phone conversations short when she is pressed for time. I always know where I stand with her, yet I *never* feel diminished or dismissed.

She has an intense executive job, is a leader in her community and involves herself in several voluntary projects. Everyone who encounters her feels valued, appreciated, and understood. We all agree that she is very nice indeed.

But people don't always use the word nice with positive intent. How many times have you heard someone say, 'She's a nice person, but ...?' I'll bet your heart sinks a little (like mine does). The phrase and the oft-associated eye roll is a backhanded compliment. The speaker suggests that the woman to whom they are referring is bland, safe, unobjectionable, *and* unsuccessful.

From childhood, society requires girls to play nicely. They need to be people pleasers and avoid disappointing other people, including parents, grandparents, friends, and teachers. Little girls stick with the game plan; they don't rock the boat. They carry this people pleasing into adulthood and their relationships at work and home. Women are labelled 'too nice'. People tell them to stop being walked over, exploited and disregarded.

The definition of a nice person is good-natured and kind. Like me, women in the 'too nice brigade' will be pleased to read that this definition doesn't spell the death knell of leadership or ambition. Niceness enhances leadership. Good-natured leaders achieve more from their direct reports. Their staff *want* to work with them because they like them, and they don't create a culture of fear or bullying.

Jack Zenger, bestselling author, speaker, and international columnist, and Joseph Folkman, a renowned psychometrician, found that friendly leaders who also set the bar high had the highest engagement levels. They called these two approaches 'drivers' and 'enhancers'. In their *Harvard Business Review* article, *Nice or tough: Which approach engages employees most?* they said, 'In our view, the lesson then is that those of you who consider yourself to be drivers should not be afraid to be the "nice guy". And all of you aspiring nice guys should not view that as incompatible with setting demanding goals'.

Lois P Frankel's book, *Nice girls don't get the corner office,* changed how we think about the word nice. Frankel argued that women are taught from childhood to seek sympathy rather than respect and influence, and women do better when they stop focusing on being liked.

Rachel Hollis carried this argument further in *Girl, stop apologizing.* (I need to declare I have a visceral reaction to both these book titles in their use of the word 'girl' instead of 'woman'. Ugh.) Hollis wrote that girls are socialised to crave approval from male authority figures in a patriarchal society. Girls want to fit in with peers. Nice girls don't discuss money, wealth or ambition for fear of being seen as selfish.

I feel sad that these books' legacy could be that nice does not equate to success, especially for women (not the authors' intent). If this is the lasting impression women take from Frankel and Hollis, it is flawed thinking.

For all the books and articles telling women to toughen up, dress more like men, and (God forbid) avoid touching their hair, there's a backlash. Women I meet have become sick and tired of this advice, and they want to demonstrate their ambition in their unique manner.

The behaviours that gain respect include kindness, concern for others and self-care. Yes, being kind to self is essential.

In my work with teams, I ask people to identify the traits they look for in their leaders. People use words such as feeling heard, valued, respected, trusted, and nurtured. They like to work for people who have a sense of purpose, good values, and an interest in the community. They want to see kindness in their leader's interactions.

It sounds to me like they identify leaders who are nice to be around. Given these people are in senior leadership roles, I assume they don't lack ambition or drive.

There will always be people who consider niceness to be a weakness. While I can't change how they think, I can help you to adjust your language.

 Reframing Exercise 5—Step One

(There is a second step later in the chapter.)

Grab a notepad or journal and a pen. Draw two columns on a page. In the first column, make a list of all the positive words you associate with nice. Leave the second column blank for now.

I acknowledge it is hard to maintain a positive focus on the word nice. There are still many examples in the media that suggest being nice makes you a pushover. When you feel affected by this, take a moment to reflect on New Zealand's Prime Minister. Jacinda Ardern won a landslide election at the end of 2020 and is one of the most popular leaders the country has seen. Ardern is a woman I consider to be nice. I also recognise and relate to her strong ambition.

Ambition is the new attractive

Meryl is a first-time founder and CEO of her own company (an accounting firm for e-commerce businesses). Meryl is ambitious; her goal is to make her firm a leading company nationally. She spends over $1,500 a month on business coaching, mastermind groups, and other support to grow her expertise. Meryl is focused and disciplined. She avoids working on too many projects at once as this is something she knows will undermine her confidence and take her into wistful thinking.

Meryl's mentor challenged her to raise her fees to four times her starting price and provide clients with a service guarantee. Meryl discovered a desire to diversify her products, and she got help to raise capital for expansion. Had Meryl never invested in herself, she said she would always have wondered how successful the startup could have been.

Meryl's ambition and determination have drawn new clients to her. Her aim to be among the best is infectious. She is an example of a woman who acted with her internal locus of control and was proactive in ensuring her business succeeded.

Meryl is the definition of ambition; she has a strong desire to achieve success and a clear intention to meet a goal. Unfortunately, we have bastardised this word too. In the western world, at least, ambition has a gendered differential. I want to shift this view with some new examples.

The traditional view of women's ambition is a turn-off. Ambition is the place for nasty girls who'll step on anyone to get what they want. 'Women sit on the razor's edge of ambition and likeability', according to Sheryl Sandberg. Sandberg is the author of the worldwide bestseller, *Lean in*.

Ambition is often viewed as a male trait. Men are encouraged to show their ambition and drive. Many articles wax lyrical about men's determination and its attractiveness. Male ambition is even described as an aphrodisiac to women. The reverse is said to be true for women. The top 12 results from my Google search 'ambition is attractive in women' were about how good ambition is for MEN (!). There were two results about why women should change their views about ambition or modify their behaviours. See a pattern here?

A second Google search about 'women and goal setting' caused the internet to overheat to thermonuclear levels. I found thousands of articles. Both Rachel Hollis' book, *Girl, stop apologizing*, referred to earlier, and Dr Debra Condren's, *Ambition is not a dirty word,* deal with women's ambition through goal setting. Condren reminds us that ambition is a virtue, not a vice. It is good for us to want to be the best we can be.

If women (and men) don't discuss their ambitions, we all suffer. The world needs humanity to be ambitious to achieve good things for the planet. It will help if we can be nice to one another in the process. Conflict hasn't got us far to date.

Reece Witherspoon penned an essay for *Glamour* magazine in 2017, following her November 2015 speech at Glamour's Women of the Year gala dinner. The address went viral when Witherspoon said the words, 'I believe ambition is not a dirty word'. Witherspoon is a Hollywood star. If you won't take it from me, listen to her, and channel your inner Elle Woods (Witherspoon's character in the *Legally Blonde* movies).

When stripped back to its basic definition, ambition means a strong desire to do or achieve something. This sounds different to how the word is used to criticise or belittle women. When power and influence are related to impact and effectiveness, women's achievements are easily demonstrated. When we reframe our language, it enables us to celebrate rather than deflect—as Witherspoon does in her *Glamour* article.

> **Reframing Exercise 6—Step Two**
>
> Accept that there will be times when your ambition will disrupt you and others. If it feels like the critics are winning, go back to your page with the two columns.
>
> Use the second column now to write all the positive words you associate with ambition.

Self-doubt may emerge. You could find yourself falling back into old thought patterns that ambition isn't a positive thing. You now have a one-page reframing tool allowing you to refocus when these thoughts strike.

Straightening your self-talk

One of my author colleagues, Jacqui, is a woman I admire for her ability to straighten out her self-talk. In a recent exchange, Jacqui shared that her inner critic had been 'rolling its eyes and clicking its tongue' telling Jacqui her book draft wasn't hitting the mark.

Jacqui was able to take on board the gifts her inner critic offered her. She went on to say, 'It has taught me much about managing the other bullies I have encountered in life'. (Now, that's a reframe to be proud of, Jacqui.)

Her negative, tut-tutting self-doubt could not thwart Jacqui's ambition to publish her next book. By keeping sight of how many women her book would inspire, Jacqui didn't give in to her inner critic. She invited it to explain itself instead so that she could learn.

Like Jacqui, when women move beyond their shame about ambition and stop people pleasing, things change. Their inner dialogue shifts. I'll show you how by reviewing what I covered in Chapter One.

Wistful thoughts come from an external locus of control. Such thoughts keep women passive and stop them from pursuing their goals. They let outside events block their progress, they maintain feelings of helplessness, and they believe they are victims of circumstance.

Worthy thoughts come from an internal locus of control. These thought patterns keep women proactive and help them maintain momentum and self-efficacy. Feeling empowered means they understand they control their destiny.

Julian Rotter developed the Locus of Control theory in the 1950s. Rotter hypothesised that people have different beliefs about how much control they have over life circumstances. Are we the victims of fate, or do we have agency over our own decisions and actions? Rotter argued that people with an external locus of control blame external influences. Those with an internal locus of control believe they influence events and outcomes themselves.

Therefore, having an internal locus of control matters. It helps women maintain worthy thinking and be proactive about their goals. If you have tended towards an external locus of control for most of your life, it is hard to transition to a new way of thinking. Your self-talk will be absolute: for example, 'This will never work for me' or 'I always fail at this stuff'.

It doesn't have to be this way. You now understand why an internal locus of control is essential and how it will help you stay focused on your ambitions. Try a locus of control test. There are several available for free on the internet. If taking an online test feels like pop psychology, you can watch a video about the locus of control and learned helplessness from the Khan Academy (see references). If you're keen to go deeper on this theme or are still sceptical, there are plenty of great resources about the topic and Rotter's early work. You don't have to take my word for it.

Let's wrap this up

This chapter has dispelled myths about women's ambitions. I have told you a story about niceness and ambition playing together, and how they can become best friends. It's possible to be ambitious and nice at the same time; it's a powerful combination for women. I have offered you a reframing exercise and further resources to expand your thinking.

Dropping old stereotypes is hard work. I don't expect you to unlearn your thought patterns overnight. It has taken you many years to learn them. Practise your worthy language. Notice when you hear other women use language revealing their wistful self-talk. Now you know about it, you will be more alert.

Review the exercises and take note of any additional ideas or thoughts that emerge. Reflect on those and any actions you might need to take as a result.

In the next chapter, I will cover why connecting with other women matters and why you're a worthy woman for others to meet. Let's help you get out there and ensure you don't hide your brilliance away.

CHAPTER SIX

Connection builds capacity

A 5-decade-long friendship that began with a phone call is an excellent title for a story about a friendship between the late US Supreme Court Justice, Ruth Bader Ginsburg (often known by her initials RBG) and Nina Totenberg. Totenberg is National Public Radio's (NPR) legal affairs reporter. She published her recollections in an obituary to Ginsburg on NPR's website. The friendship started with a telephone call back in 1971, when Totenberg wanted to ask Ginsburg a question about a legal brief she had authored. Their hour-long conversation was the first of many and began a long professional and personal connection.

Women gain power, inspiration and vitality from one another; sometimes they gain friendship too. Women are more creative and energised by each other when they have common interests—like RBG and Totenberg. Data shows that women who collaborate with other women achieve more and faster. Women who place themselves at the centre of their network gain access to introductions, opportunities, and learning. It's not mercenary or selfish. It's sensible.

Some women worry about networking. When their managers ask them to attend events, they shudder. They feel they are not interesting enough or have nothing of value to add to conversations—as was the case for one woman I met at a workshop. She had managed to avoid every invitation to attend industry conferences over many years. She admitted to me that she was frightened to participate on her own because she didn't know how to 'do networking'. The story from Totenberg shows that 'doing networking' doesn't have to involve hundreds of people. Women can connect for capacity-building on a scale that suits them.

But, for women to succeed and thrive, they have to adopt a new way of thinking. According to the authors of *Stretch: How to future-proof yourself for tomorrow's workplace*, people need to focus on three imperatives. Karie Willyerd and Barbara Mistick suggest workers of the future need the ability to think in any situation. First, people need to feel like they are in control (a neat loop back to the locus of control discussion in Chapter Five). Second, workers should give themselves options and broaden their horizons. Third, they should set goals and be open to new experiences and networks, and learning new skills.

Chapter Five asked you to make two columns on a piece of paper (one each for worthy words to define 'nice' and 'ambitious'). This exercise focused on reframing language to help you stay positive. Another way to build your future capacity is to surround yourself with women who help you—as Willyerd and Mistick show.

Willyerd is the senior vice president and chief learning officer for Visa. She has written two books on the future of work based on her knowledge of learning and development from her extensive career with multi-national companies. Mistick is the Washington-based president of the National Association of Independent Colleges and Universities—the largest organisation representing independent, non-profit colleges and universities in the USA. She has a long career within learning organisations. Their ideas are worthy of attention. It's clear then that networks are a powerful accessory for people's careers. Networks are like the favourite handbag you take everywhere because it holds all the stuff you must have.

There are many and varied networks in existence. There's one right for you. Valerie Khoo espoused the benefits of sampling many networks in her 2011 article, *The truth about the new business women's networks*, for *The Sydney Morning Herald*. Khoo described the rapid growth of women-specific networks across the country and advised women to explore several to determine the right fit for purpose and need.

Collaboration creates change

At the start of any new women's group program with a company, I conduct one-on-one interviews with each participant. These brief conversations reveal what women want most from employer-sponsored programs. The women in one group gave me these insights into their needs. They wanted to:

- Understand themselves and their unique leadership styles.
- Celebrate their existing achievements.
- Be with like-minded women to keep them motivated and positive.

Don't underestimate the power of women supporting each other at work. So says Anne Welsh McNulty in her article of the same name for *Harvard Business Review* in 2018.

While discussing the value of women's support organisations, Welsh McNulty said:

'These [research and leadership development opportunities] are wonderful supplements, but they can't replace the benefits of and the necessity for connections among women inside a company — at and across all levels. It reduces the feeling of competition for an imaginary quota at the top'.

Organisations worldwide invest in women's group mentoring programs because they know such programs accelerate women's career progression. While research shows that diversity programs alone won't lead to promotions, they connect women to a support structure to scaffold their development.

Women make career progress faster through networks and groups than they do alone. In part, this is because it is easier to maintain an internal locus of control and stay positive when they have other women in their corner. The benefits are mutual and reciprocal, like the women in my group programs seek.

The capacity and willingness of women to support each other is why women's networking groups flourish. Women want to help each other. Most women's networks offer opportunities to learn new skills. Yet there's no need to be involved in everything. Time is limited. Many networks operate online—even more since the COVID-19 pandemic created the need for physical distancing. For example, Latrobe Women in Business, based in Gippsland, ran several online events in 2020. Committee members told me their events reached more women across the region than before the pandemic.

They connected farther and broader, enabling local women to meet with speakers like Carolyn Creswell, Founder of Carman's Kitchen, television presenter, and 2012 Australian Business Woman of the Year.

I rarely hear women say they haven't found a network helpful. I have not found any data to suggest women's networks do anything other than amplify support to their members. As the evidence in this chapter shows, the consensus among researchers is that networks help all people to achieve more and faster.

As discussed earlier, women are programmed people pleasers. Being liked is a primal need. But it's impossible to make friends with everybody—it's a fact of life. And nobody is asking you to connect with every woman you meet. Choose your network to ensure you connect to people with whom you have shared values. When you do this, you won't notice the people who are the exceptions. You'll be too busy having a good time and sharing the great stuff you know.

Find out about women's networks near you. There might be one in your workplace. As Valerie Khoo suggests, make a list of networks to explore. Then, read *10 ways to support and empower the women in your life this year* by Sharon Green on the She Defined website.

One barrier is knowing where to start with your network. Don't let your lack of awareness about networks thwart your progress. Ask your friends, check social media and ask around the office. People *will* help you.

Are you thinking that you should be able to look after your career by yourself? Or that self-reliance is a sign of maturity and asking for help makes you look vulnerable and uncertain? Think again. Imagine another woman in your circle reached out to you for an introduction to someone you know well. You'd be happy to help. You wouldn't see her as weak and vulnerable. **You're worthy of support too.**

Networks build nations

On 9 October 2012, a little girl sat on a bus in the Swat Valley region of Pakistan. She had just taken an exam and was on her way home from school. A gunman boarded the bus and shot her along with two other girls in an assassination attempt. He didn't think she was worthy of an education, let alone the chance to change the world.

The victim, Malala Yousafzai, woke up ten days later in a hospital in Birmingham, England. Malala, as she is universally known, became the youngest Nobel Prize laureate after she went on to found the Malala Fund with her father in 2013. Through Mr Yousafzai's networks and the help of well-connected people, the

Malala Fund now works in Afghanistan, Brazil, Ethiopia, India, Lebanon, Nigeria, Pakistan and Turkey. The fund's main aim is to enable more than 130 million girls worldwide to access secondary education in countries that deny it to them.

Malala's example is extreme. Yet she is living proof that networks boost development through collective advocacy and community action.

Some women don't enjoy networking. Some say they hate it. Is it introversion? Or could it be because they feel like they have nothing worth sharing with the people they might meet? Might they be judged as 'not enough'? As not intelligent, interesting, or important enough to meet?

Here's a secret. I used to be one of those women. The thought of networking for the sake of it chilled my blood. I'm shy and reserved by nature. My instincts are to recharge by having time on my own. And when I was younger, I felt I had no place in the company of people who seemed more important, articulate, and accomplished than me. Going to events to network with other people has been hard for me in the past. At times, it still is.

Carol Stewart, career coach, author of *Quietly visible*, and one of the top-four LinkedIn Voices in the United Kingdom, acknowledges three things that happen for introverts who force themselves to wear an extroverted mask when with other people: exhaustion, diminished self-belief, and a feeling of not being good enough. In her LinkedIn article, *3 consequences when introverted women leaders put on an extroverted persona*, Stewart advises not to pretend to be somebody else but to manage energy levels and be authentic.

My work life has meant I have had to adapt and learn to engage with groups of people from diverse backgrounds. These people include governors-general and governors, prime ministers and premiers, departmental secretaries, senior clergy, corporate leaders, and more. Later in this chapter, I will share my hacks.

What helped me get over my resistance to networking and meeting new people? What took away the fear? **Purpose.**

I found it more manageable when I could see the greater good behind the event I was asked to attend, for example, a fundraiser for a charity. I could walk into a room full of other people and have a sense of shared intent. This shared objective gave me a topic to talk about when I met people. It helped to get conversations started.

Over the many years I have practised networking, I have become better at it. I no longer baulk at different types of events. I now understand how connecting with like-minded people helps my sense of self-worth and encourages me to keep investing in my growth.

This shift enabled me to join a service club. In 2006, I joined Rotary International, an organisation that provides 16 million volunteer hours each year worldwide. Rotary causes include:

- Promoting peace.
- Fighting disease.
- Providing clean water.
- Saving mothers and children.
- Supporting education.
- Growing local economies.
- Protecting the environment.

Highlights of my involvement are funding the construction of a well for a remote community in Indonesia in partnership with an all-women Rotary Club in Bali, and becoming the first woman president of my club.

Women have access to outstanding and diverse opportunities when they join networks with a values base. Women like me, who find networking difficult, can learn to manage it when they have a reason to give their time.

The feel-good factor of community service is positive for mental health. The *Greater Good Magazine* from the Berkeley University of California featured an article, *How volunteering can help your mental health*, by Elizabeth Hopper. The article discussed research cited in the *Journal of Happiness Studies*. Around 70,000 people in the United Kingdom were surveyed about their volunteerism and their capacity to function well. Researchers assessed the group every two years between 1996 and 2014. People who had volunteered in the past year said they were more satisfied with their lives and health than those who hadn't.

Consider the local community activists and leaders you know. Are they doing something that sparks your interest? Networking with purpose is good for the world—and you. You are worthy of making a difference.

Still not convinced? Networking with a social purpose may not be your style. Reflect on your values. There *will* be something to nudge you. Think of something involving your children or partner—being part of a network that enhances your family time might help you commit to the cause.

Fear of lacking specific expertise or knowledge about a cause stops some people from offering support. We all start at our beginning. There are lots of ways to help that don't require in-depth knowledge of a subject. Showing up and helping is valued. You might start by offering to bring the coffee orders.

Learn to network, even when you hate it

Earlier, I promised to share my tips on how to make networking easier when you loathe it. Before I do, here's some bonus advice for women who want to improve their networking skills.

CHAPTER SIX: CONNECTION BUILDS CAPACITY

Get help from an expert. I did. And so do many influential and leading women I know. We don't expect to do this alone.

It's who you know is an international bestselling book. Published twice, in several languages, the premise of Janine Garner's book is connection. Many of my coaching and mentoring clients are gifted a copy, and I include it in goodie bags I provide at women's workshops.

Working with Janine Garner has taught me the power of 'Hot' networks. Garner's Networking Matrix™ program teaches the differences between Hot, Warm and Cold connections and why this distinction matters. When women network with people they already know (their 'Hot' connections) with a clear purpose in mind, they progress further and faster. They can then access introductions to 'Warm' contacts—people known to their friends and colleagues. There's no need to spend hours attending large events connecting to a 'Cold' network. Occasionally, for a specific reason (like an inspiring speaker), is all it takes.

So, women who seek support and expertise get better at networking. Connection with an existing network or building a new one doesn't need to fill women with feelings of dread.

I want women who read this book to make the most of networking and find it more comfortable. I want readers to feel like they can't wait to dive into their development and view networking as one tool to help them.

Some years ago, Donna McGeorge, an author friend and colleague, introduced me to the idea of JOMO (the Joy of Missing Out). It is the opposite of the Fear of Missing Out or FOMO.

When women embrace JOMO, they cherish their time. They attend the activities that bring the most energy. They look for ways to benefit others and add the most to other women's experiences. And their self-worth skyrockets as a result.

You won't enjoy all events and activities. I don't wish to convince you to love networking. Yet there is a way to make the most of almost every networking event you attend and to feel like you've made a worthwhile contribution while you're there.

Kath Walters, author, book coach and renowned Australian business journalist, designs questions to inspire, create interest, and generate an outcome. Kath advises that questions work best when there's a statement of purpose up-front and when questioners seek permission to ask. When I sought Kath's assistance to enhance my questioning techniques, she helped me design questions I could use when networking. Below are some I like.

- One of the things I notice at these events is that I want to go beyond the small talk. I find people so interesting. Would it be okay if I asked you a question about yourself?

- I'm here to meet people I wouldn't usually get to meet. It doesn't come naturally to me. How about you?

- I'm a curious person. Is it okay if I ask you some questions about you?

- I can tell I might need some of your expertise. What I know is that it usually takes me a couple of questions to clarify my thoughts. Is it okay if I ask you a couple?

When women prepare questions in advance, they can focus on conversations with ease. They meet the individuals they need to meet. Plans take away some of the nerves and feelings of inadequacy.

 Exercise 7

Design three questions of your own that you can have on hand for your next networking event. At the end of the

> chapter, read *Six ways to hack your networking nerves*. You don't need to master all the hacks. Choose one to practise. Then adopt some of the others as you grow braver.

And don't put networking on hold until the kids are older. It matters now, and it can be fun.

Let's wrap this up

Women benefit as individuals and as a collective when they collaborate, and they can enhance each other's collective self-worth. Cooperation can occur in small, focused groups or more extensive networks.

Women's networks matter. Networks help women develop new skills and make connections. Women learn more when they network with a purpose and goal in mind.

Introverted women can learn to enjoy networking—or at least to not hate it.

Don't chastise yourself about your dislike or fear of networking. Use the hacks provided to create an experience you enjoy. **You are worthy of investing time in connecting with other women.** Don't let your lack of knowledge or comfort get in your way.

Research the women's networks available to you. Consider local community projects to energise you and increase your feelings of self-worth.

Chapter Seven looks at how wistful self-talk keeps women in jobs they no longer love. Long-term loyalty to an employer might not serve women well. Women need to know what to do when it's time to leave, and I'll give you my insights to help you decide.

Six ways to hack your networking nerves

1. DOUBLE THE DELIGHT. If there's an event that you want to attend, but you're an avoider, book two tickets. Take a friend, a colleague or your mentee / mentor. It's much easier when you're not alone, and you get to treat someone to a pleasant experience with you.

2. EARLY ENTRY. Ensure you arrive early. If you're among the first people to walk in, other guests have no option but to meet you. Stand near the refreshments table or the registration desk, smile, and people will chat with you. You won't be breaking into an existing group or feeling quite so awkward.

3. COVET THE CORNERS. Look at the corners of the room—that's where the quieter, more introverted folks are likely to be. Chances are they will be in a small group, maybe even alone. Make a beeline for them and introduce yourself. If they look bewildered and nervous, you get to help them feel more comfortable.

4. REHEARSE YOUR REPERTOIRE. Have a set of questions that you can draw upon in any situation. These are questions that you have practised in advance so they come naturally to you.

5. JUMP FOR JOMO! It's okay to say 'no' sometimes. You can opt for the Joy of Missing Out. You don't have to go to every single networking event. Pick a handful that inspire you. If it's a three-day conference and you spend one night

having room service and early lights out, nobody will notice. You're welcome!

6. POWER YOUR PURPOSE. Have a purpose for attending a networking event. Master Sales Trainer, Rachel Bourke, never goes to an event without her goals at the forefront of her mind. Rachel is a champion networker and enjoys meeting people. Be like Rachel. Have your goals clear before you book for the event. They might go something like this:

- I will meet three new people whom I've never met before.
- I will learn one new thing about a colleague that I'd not known prior.
- I will take away an idea for collaboration in my industry sector or my organisation.

These goals help you focus on the sorts of conversations you want to have and the individuals you want to meet.

* Here's a special note for conference attendance, especially if it's the first time you have attended a conference by yourself.

- When you receive the conference pack by email or online, check the list of delegates. Make a note of the people you know or with whom you are associated.
- Once you have selected them, send an email or a personal message on LinkedIn to tell them you will be attending. Ask them what they are most looking forward to at the conference and suggest you meet on arrival. Use this email / message to practise some of the questions you added to your toolkit. You will be surprised how this gets the conversation established.

- People appreciate that you have reached out, especially those who might be feeling like you.
- When you do this in advance of a conference, you arrive knowing there are already people who will be looking out for you.

CHAPTER SEVEN

Hit the road, Jill

Every spring in Victoria, we see advertisements across the media telling us to prepare our fire plans. Before summer, we are not at immediate risk of fire. Yet the emergency services urge us to clean up our homes, pack important documents and be ready to flee. Advertising tells us to be alert for signs of fire. We know what to do when a fire comes.

Think of this chapter like your fire plan for exiting your job when you no longer love it … when your itchy feet are annoying you. I have based this chapter on the mentoring work I do with women. Women who want more. Women who have fallen out of love with their work.

You've made your professional development investment plan. You've stirred your ambition. You know you're ready for responsibility. So, what's next?

Should you leave your current job? Deep down, you know when it's time to move on. But wistful thoughts keep women from resigning from their jobs. Even when they know they should. Women risk staying in jobs due to a sense of loyalty—not because they get satisfaction and joy from their work. When you're disengaged, long-term commitment doesn't serve your employer either. If your heart isn't in the job anymore, you are being unfair by staying.

You might not feel this right now, but when the time comes will you recognise the signs? Will you know what to do? Or will you forget your worthy self-talk and get stuck?

Hanging on too long in one job can derail your career. Staying may mean sacrifice. Women need to know how to identify when the magic at work has gone. This knowledge helps them to ascertain if it's time to leave.

The transition to a new job might take time. It won't be linear and it's essential to exit with elegance. Knowing how to leave well is a skill that worthy women have.

The sacrifice of staying

'Kara' has stayed 20 years in her job. Some people applaud her loyalty. I don't. It bugs me. Here's why. Kara told me she feels lost, stuck, and *stranded*. One internal voice tells her to stay. The hours are good. She has the flexibility to work from home sometimes. She has time with her kids. The money is excellent.

But Kara's other internal voice tells her different things. This voice reminds her that she has never once had a performance review. She doesn't get to discuss pay rises or bonuses for the new work she brings in, despite asking several times.

Kara is bored witless. The job has become mundane, and there's no longer a challenge. She doesn't enjoy supervising her team. She blames her team for how she feels. In her gut, she knows the problem isn't her team and she also knows it's not all her employer's fault.

It's Kara. She has fallen out of love with her job.

How on earth has she allowed herself to stay so long? What's stopping her from leaving? Loyalty to a boss she respects? Yes. Fear of change? Probably.

CHAPTER SEVEN: HIT THE ROAD, JILL

Even Kara's parents have told her they notice how listless she is. She's unhappy and confused, and she feels she's left it too late to change.

I don't want you to experience this. I want you to know how to fix it. **And I want you to feel worthy enough to do so.**

'Job-clingers' face several risks. According to Terina Allen, consultant and speaker, job-clingers are people who have stayed more than five years in one job with no change in title, job responsibilities or salary, and no shifts in the company to gain new skills. Allen identifies the risks for job-clingers as:

1. Weakened chances of promotion.
2. Lower pay (in that most of us get a pay rise of one to three per cent per annum if we stay in the same job but could increase that dramatically if we moved).
3. Becoming less visible and relevant to senior management.

Allen's points are stark and confronting; they seem like sure-fire ways to undermine worthy thoughts. That is why women need to be able to identify when it's time to leave. When women are no longer captivated, that feeling is telling them something crucial, for example, it is time to end the relationship.

Women risk the sacrifices of learning opportunities, growth, and meeting new people when they stay too long. The most significant forfeit is the thrill of a challenge. When every day is the same, it eats away at you. Your negative feelings about work affect more people than you. Your family and friendships suffer too. Making a change is for your happiness and you're worthy of being happy.

What's my evidence? It's the premise of the whole book. If this chapter resonates with you, I'm pleased. It's why I'm writing it.

Contrast Kara with another woman I know.

'Bridie' left her organisation after 19 years. She had worked in a range of related jobs, and after this long period, she decided to change industries. People have already remarked to her how vibrant she is, how happy she seems and how empowered she has become. Bridie feels brave. She feels worthy. Bridie got clear on her values and what matters to her in life. And she went searching for a role to match.

When people are bored at work, the impact is dramatic, according to Melissa Lamson. Lamson is a global leadership expert and the president and CEO of Lamson Consulting. In her article for *Inc.com, You're not burnt-out. You're bored-out,* Lamson writes about people who dread going to work each day. Every day is the same, and the job has lost its challenge. Lamson says boredom at work can create feelings just like burnout or what she calls bored-out.

Even if you're bored, like Kara, you might believe there are no other jobs with the conditions you want and need. Possibly. It's a fair point to raise. But have you looked? Often the women I meet have the same excuse. Yet, when we unpack their beliefs, they've never stopped to explore what else is possible.

Kara's and Bridie's stories are examples of how different perspectives lead to different outcomes. Bridie investigated and found what she was looking for. It didn't happen straight away. Over several months, she worked on her action plan and stayed clear about what she wanted to achieve.

You can do it too. There's a balance of course. While staying too long can mean sacrifice, leaving too soon can affect your reputation.

When scanning résumés, a question will emerge in an employer's mind if they see one showing a different job every few months, especially if there's no clear explanation as to why. For example, if you are a contractor or a temp work specialist, it's apparent why you've moved, for others though, swapping jobs in fast succession suggests you have no staying power. Your ability to commit to a project and see it through comes under question.

But this chapter is for women who are clinging on for long periods, such as eight to ten years or more—the women who no longer feel the buzz that drew them to the job in the first place.

 Exercise 8

Which of these, if any, do you notice in yourself at work?

- Fighting against changes and new ideas.
- A lack of stimulation and feeling bored.
- Being critical of others.
- Feeling cynical about the organisation and its leadership.
- Feeling mismatched to your job.
- You can do your job efficiently, yet you underperform because you can't be bothered.

Did you tick any? If you ticked three or more, what does this mean for you?

You might now have a sensation in your stomach. The visceral reaction we have when stuff is hard to face. It can feel scary.

I didn't pose this question to make you feel worse. I want to help you identify what's eating at you and help you plan for something new.

I often ask my coaching clients to complete a longer exercise on this theme. Some of them find it unsettling as it brings forth buried feelings of dissatisfaction at work.

There's a well-known saying I'm sure you've heard many times: the best learning comes when we lean into discomfort. Persevere with the questions and notice what they draw out from you. It's all good learning.

Change can be clunky

Henriette Rothschild stepped down from 16 years at the Hay Group (now the KornFerry HayGroup). At the time, she had been the managing director, Pacific for more than six years. Rothschild shared her views in a LinkedIn article in 2016. She wrote it was the most challenging decision she ever made in her role. According to Rothschild,

> To do this role well, it would take at least a further three or four years. That would mean I would have been in the same role for ten years: not a good outcome for the organisation or me. It got me thinking: why is this decision to leave so hard? Fear of the unknown, the risk of (potential) income reduction and loss of status are common reasons why someone may choose not to leave. However, I felt for me the reasons were more deep-seated. As a child and through education, the value of 'finish what you start' was a strong one: you have to master a skill before you take on the next challenge. Also the fear of letting down the team. But this childhood lesson doesn't always serve us well when the organisations we lead are constantly evolving, and the job is never finished or even mastered.

Rothchild's is a powerful story about how hard it can be to leave a job. She articulates the complex set of reasons that stop women from moving on.

If senior global executives struggle with this choice, what about the rest of us?

The mistake women often make is thinking a career transition will be undeviating and easy. From childhood, women are conditioned to believe climbing up is the only direction to go when they change jobs. It is this belief that stops women from moving.

When women trust they are worthy of loving their work, they can move in directions other than upwards. They can see different ways to progress and develop. To quote Whitney Johnson, author of *Disrupt yourself*,

> I think the biggest misconception is that when we look back on it, it looks very, very linear and yet, the reality is you go up and then you step back. And then you go up and then you step back. And you go up and you step back. And I think it's rare that when we're making a transition that we're able to just go from step to step to step. Almost always there's a step back in order to slingshot forward.

Harvard Business Review interviewed Johnson in a podcast in 2018. Her words about career transitions could not be more relevant here.

Change also requires courage. Courage to be patient, yet not for too long. Women need to be brave to identify the best transition for themselves. Bravery helps women ask questions like those in Exercise 8.

A tip: it is useful to remind yourself that you don't need to leap immediately or in an unexpected way. It's not like a rebound relationship after a break-up. You don't need to date the first person who asks you. Courage to be curious means you seek to understand the experiences of others. Hear what they have learned and how you might apply these insights.

In his book, *The purpose path: A guide to pursuing your authentic life's work*, Dr Nicholas Pearce discusses building a life and work of significance. He calls this 'vocational courage'. I love this phrase. It is the most potent description I have read and has a depth of application to who we are as humans. Pearce is a scholar, speaker, entrepreneur, and pastor. He is a management and organisation professor at the Northwestern University Kellogg School of Management and founder and CEO of The Vocati Group. Pearce's writing goes beyond the meaning of work. Vocational courage is finding and pursuing a real purpose in life and making sure a life's work is reflected in daily tasks.

Even after reading this section, you might still be feeling like Kara. You're pushing back against all the evidence. Your inner voice says what you have in your current job can't be replicated anywhere else. You tell yourself you're trapped and must stay. It's your call. You're in control. But keep yourself in check. Are you being a martyr? Are you avoiding change and discomfort? If you're speaking in absolutes again, your locus of control has left the room and gone external. It is keeping you the victim in your drama.

When people are uncertain, it can be tempting to leap back to the familiar. Some women return to a workplace where they once felt at ease and liked their job. Be cautious and forewarned about this move. It can backfire. I once coached a woman who did this. She had been in an administration role for many years with one employer. She left to change careers and sectors. This move didn't work out well for her. She returned to her old workplace, seeking what she knew. She won a more senior managerial role. Most of her former colleagues were still there. They continued to relate to her as her past self (as if she were in her old job). She felt she couldn't move on because *they* couldn't or wouldn't. Her male, more senior colleagues were tone-deaf when she tried talking with them about how this affected her. And to be fair, she wasn't clear with them about what she needed.

 Exercise 9

Answer these questions:

- Name three jobs you would enjoy that take you sideways rather than up.
- Which jobs would you like to try? Do they have more scope or a better salary but with a less senior title?

> - When you open your mind and imagine you could work anywhere, doing anything, what pictures emerge?
> - What time frame do you need for this to happen?
>
> Did you discover anything interesting? I hope you feel energised and inspired. I hope you feel powerful and worthy.

Make notes of the answers to these questions. Keep those notes handy. New thoughts will pop up at the most inconvenient times. When they do, record them on your phone using the voice recorder option. I want you to have access to this information, and the feelings you notice, when you need it most (after a rough day at work.)

Exit with elegance

After 15 years in the company (and straight out of university), 'Rosie' sought a total shift. When she reviewed her values, she recognised she had changed over those years. So had the things Rosie desired for her life and her work. Rosie told her manager when she noticed these feelings. She explained how she planned to research her next steps a full year before her departure. This extended conversation began at her performance review. It enabled Rosie to achieve maximum support from her direct line manager and her next level executive. When she left, Rosie was at peace with her decision and excited for her future—all with full blessing from the colleagues she valued most.

Knowing how to leave a job well is a skill worth having. I want women to rock, not ruin, their resignation when the time comes. Women don't have to leave their jobs under a cloud or with regrets. They don't need to burn bridges. Reputation matters when resigning from a position. Making a graceful exit keeps women highly regarded and remembered for the right reasons. When women don't leave well, their reputations suffer. They feel less confident, and their departing actions may plague them. They will be rueful and find the feeling hard to shake.

There are three steps to an elegant exit.

1. No surprises, only transparency.

    Be like Rosie and let your manager know in advance how you're feeling. Use your performance review discussions as a temperature check about whether you are still satisfied at work. Performance reviews are not merely for development planning.

2. No grudges, only gratitude.

    There are things about this job you don't like, that's a given. Focus on what you *have* enjoyed, what you've learned and what you've brought to the company, not just what you've taken.

3. No maligning, only reflections.

    Don't 'can the joint' when you're leaving. It's unfair to infect your colleagues with your sour grapes or frustrations. Follow the adage that if you've got nothing nice to say, say nothing. Remember, it was your choice to stay so long. It's not everybody else's responsibility. Besides, you never know when you might need to call on a favour or ask for a reference.

Are you left wondering if all these steps will matter in the long run?

You're worthy of putting in the time and effort for an elegant exit. You're worthy of a robust reputation—one of being fair and reasonable in your dealings. Make sure your next employer knows they're getting a good catch.

Staying quiet about problems isn't always the solution, of course. If your workplace is genuinely awful and terrible things are happening, you need to share those with someone. There are laws and policies to protect you and others. Use them.

 Exercise 10

At this point, I'd like you to do something a bit different. Grab a pen and paper, and handwrite a draft resignation letter. Write it with my three tips in mind: transparency, gratitude, and reflections.

Then, imagine yourself at your farewell afternoon tea. Think about what you will say in your speech. (Yes, you *will* make one.) Visualise the process you will have put in place to avoid surprises for your manager.

These two exercises will help you recall what you like about your work and what you've learned—you might discover you want to stay after all.

It feels odd to write a letter you might not send—like the letters to your 16-year-old self as seen on social media from time to time. Push through this feeling. The value is in the reflective process and sensing how you feel.

Let's wrap this up

This chapter has shared why staying too long in a job creates complacency, depletes joy, and affects personal and work relationships. I have given you tips to help you know when it's time to seek your next job, and when you're not being fair to yourself or your employer. I have described how a transition to your next role can take time and needs planning, and I have shown why you need to make an elegant exit to enhance your reputation and embed your ethics.

Overcoming uneasy feelings that arise will be hard. The decision to leave your job is a tough one, more so if you've been avoiding it.

I hope you'll do the exercises. Be gentle with yourself, but don't give up. If you've read this far, you know you need to do this thinking.

The next chapter is for those readers who are sitting with their ambition to move into a leadership role. I'll show that women are worthy of leading and why we need more women to lead in their unique ways.

CHAPTER EIGHT

Leadership is lonely, isn't it?

You've wrapped your head around your worthiness. You've dived into your development and you've amplified your ambition. You know how to network with the people who matter most in your circle. And you've found a cause to champion in your community.

Now, you're longing for a leadership role. But your inner voice is telling you that's the wrong move.

Could you lead others? Are you well enough prepared? Are you worthy of being in charge? You've only ever heard that leadership is lonely, challenging, and scary. You might not cope with that.

Don't believe everything you hear. Leadership can be enlivening when you have a strong foundation and framework on which to lean.

This chapter outlines the tools needed in a Worthy to Lead Toolkit. I'll show how women avoid pitfalls by learning from the experiences and insights of others in their networks. I want readers to be saved from the pain of the mistakes I made by trying to lead without support.

Some years back, I took a job in another part of the state. I thought I could manage everything, including the relocation, by myself. I thought I had it nailed. In a month (and just before Christmas),

I started a new job, found accommodation, and prepared for an overseas trip. But eight weeks later, I was burned out, frazzled and regretful. My self-talk was all criticism. My inner voice said I wasn't suitable for the job, and I should resign and go home. I told myself I wasn't worthy of having this life. I don't want you or anyone else to experience such feelings.

In this chapter, I'll reveal how my clients found perseverance was possible when they connected to others and when they were curious to expand their knowledge.

Angela Duckworth believes talent is overrated. In her revolutionary book, *Grit*, Duckworth showed that perseverance and determination are more important than talent alone. These are what help us flourish in work and life. Endurance, resolve, and purpose are your keys to leading well; it's not just your talent or what you've studied.

Leaders who link with other people lead better. Connection with other leaders creates growth. Networking with purpose reduces loneliness. It opens up opportunity. Great leaders enjoy their networks, and they don't seek large numbers of people. They find the right tribe for the purpose at hand. **Women wanting to lead need to get connected.** (I showed you how in Chapter Six).

Responsibility can be rewarding in numerous ways. It's not just the financial benefits of promotion. It's the intellectual stimulation and satisfaction that comes with the job. **Women who want new responsibilities to challenge them need to get captivated.**

One of the best ways to flourish as a new leader is to ask questions. New leaders are not required to have all the answers—neither are those with experience. The most accomplished leaders ask questions. They hire people who know more about the subject matter than they do. **Women who want to manage better need to get curious.**

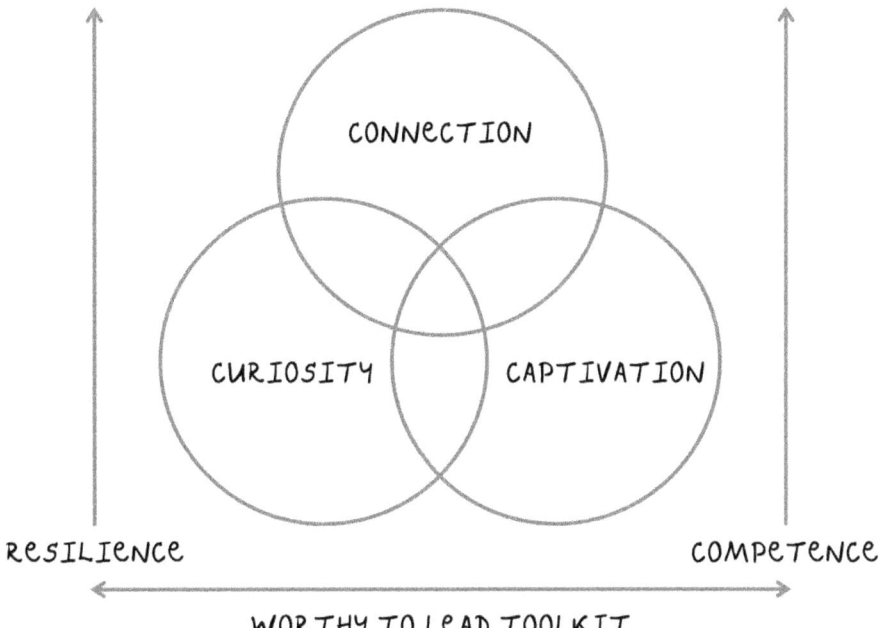

The three elements in the framework pictured—connection, captivation and curiosity—help maintain leadership resilience and grow our competence to lead.

Leadership doesn't have to be lonely

Katrina is a swim school owner and instructor in northern Victoria. She is mentored by a former Olympic coach. She connected with her coach to lead herself, lead her team, and, more importantly, grow her business. Katrina knew that by operating from a remote regional base, she couldn't flourish on her own.

Women who want to lead need to connect to other leaders. It's the first element of leadership competence and item one in the Worthy to Lead Toolkit. Humans are tribal animals. We tend to do better when we feel supported by a community of practice.

Leadership is hard if done alone and away from others. Women who think they don't need support to lead will eventually fail. Those who get connected maximise their capacity.

Stephen Covey, acclaimed author of *First things first*, identifies that we can't set our priorities without attending to our four areas of human need. Covey describes need number two as social (maintaining relationships). Expanding on this in *The 7 habits of highly effective people*, Covey says habit four is creating stable relationships with others.

Don't believe me? Then argue all you like with one of the world's greatest thinkers on connection … go your hardest.

The doubters may be thinking, *I don't know any leaders I could approach.* Unless you are self-employed, you have a manager or some form of a boss. Are your doubts based on truth or is it an external locus of control voice speaking?

Others could be thinking they'd be too embarrassed to discuss fears or a lack of knowledge. This chapter, indeed this book, is asking you to stretch yourself and up-end all the things you've heard and think you know. The best way to remedy doubts is to talk with the leaders you know and discover how they manage—don't just take my word as gospel. I bet they will say they often rely on their connections for support.

You can't always depend on other people to help you. There will be times when you need faith that you are leading well. How do leaders measure outcomes when they can't seek feedback from colleagues? Work at times requires us to be solo. Sometimes, we need to trust ourselves more. We can't always have our manager's ear straightaway.

Here are some tips on how to move from isolated to inspired. In their *Harvard Business review* article, *How to improve at work when you're not getting feedback,* Jack Zenger and Joseph Folkman discussed the ways we can know if we're doing a good job—especially when we are not getting feedback.

Zenger and Folkman outlined the following factors:

- Delivering results.
- Being a trusted co-worker.
- Having technical expertise.
- Delivering on strategy.
- Marketing your work to others.
- Motivating other people.

These are helpful benchmarks to start.

There's a further objection I often hear. Women who consider themselves to be introverts tell me they struggle with the idea of leading. It holds them back and sometimes stops them from leaning into leadership. These women believe they are unsuitable for high profile jobs. They see themselves as too shy or reserved to be a good fit. This belief has been disproven by various thought leaders.

My personal favourite is Susan Cain, an American author and academic. Cain wrote *Quiet: The power of introverts in a world that can't stop talking* and *Quiet power: The secret strengths of introverts*. Her website, Quiet Revolution, has benefitted many of my coaching clients. They have learned how to use their introversion to create what Cain describes as executive presence. Cain's work has changed many women's beliefs about themselves and their fit within a noisy world.

Make a list of the leaders you can call on for support and morale building. These are the people who have your back and will help you maintain your worthy inner voice. List a minimum of five people, including former managers, people who chair networks you belong to, and leaders you admire and know well enough to invite for coffee.

When you have five names, write (alongside them) why you chose them and what they represent to you. There will be clues about what you value in leadership and the things you might wish to emulate in your style.

As hard as this might seem at first, you **can** come up with five names. If not, humour me and write just three. Don't push back and think people won't want to support you. You'll be surprised at how generous and giving people are when you are a new leader. Remember, they've all been there themselves.

Responsibility is rewarding

'Julie' discovered how rewarding it felt to have more responsibility. She loved the intellectual stimulation of being in charge each time she acted as CEO in her workplace. Yet she stopped herself from applying for chief executive jobs every time a relevant one was advertised. She even stalled when she was approached by recruiters or boards interested in her skills.

Julie came to me for coaching because she wanted to understand the barriers she placed in front of herself. She knew she was capable of more and excited by the prospect of doing so. But Julie believed she always shot herself in the foot.

The crux came when Julie saw her perfect job advertised. To quote her, 'It had my name written all over it'. Julie decided not to apply. Her wistful inner voice told her other people were more qualified. To rub salt in the wound, Julie was invited by the hiring organisation to sit on the interview panel because of her experience and knowledge. Did Julie kick herself? You bet. At the interviews, Julie saw the candidates were less qualified and less experienced than she was.

Julie was bored with her work and needed the challenge of higher responsibility. No matter how tough leadership would be, it was tougher to stay in middle management, where she was under-utilised and becoming deskilled. Julie decided to respond to executive job ads of interest. She knew this was the solution to her frustration.

Responsibility can be rewarding in numerous ways. It's not just the financial benefits of promotion. It's the intellectual stimulation and satisfaction of the job. I call this feeling captivation.

Captivation is the second element of leadership competence and item two in your Worthy to Lead Toolkit. Working in a job we don't like is one of the biggest factors in undermining self-worth. A major cause of falling out of love with work is a lack of stimulation: being bored and unchallenged. Having responsibility for leading a project, team, or an organisation doesn't have to be framed as daunting. Responsibility can be exciting and developmental in itself. The growth gained stands women in good stead for many aspects of life.

Some women doubt this. They have heard that responsibility drains and depletes leaders. I have shown in Julie's example that to stay in a role without challenge is *more* depleting.

There are times in life when a lack of challenge is okay. When people are stretched in their personal lives, having less demands at work may be helpful. But this feeling doesn't last forever for women with ambition to do more. There comes a time when they want to test their capabilities further with more responsibility. When women understand and accept the reward from responsibility, their inner voice changes.

 Exercise 11

How captivated are you in your work? Try these questions for reflection:

- Who am I at work? Is this a different me to the person I am at home? What can I learn from this?

- What would I rather not acknowledge about myself? What blind spots affect the way I feel about my job?
- What do I enjoy most / want more of at work? What do I enjoy the least / want less of?
- What do my partner, children and friends hear from me about work?
- How can I use those insights to enhance my enjoyment in my current job or to prepare for my next job search?
- What do I want my job to achieve? What am I aiming towards?

Some of my clients find this exercise disquieting. It brings forth feelings of dissatisfaction and a desire for more. Many women try to squash such feelings, often for long periods. Persevere with the questions and notice what they draw out from you.

Curiosity creates competence

In the leadership programs I run, I teach leaders to ask, not tell. Without exception, participants who practise questioning techniques with their direct reports get improved results. Participants report less stress, increased confidence, and better solutions to problems without solving them for their staff. It is compelling data.

One of the best ways to thrive as a leader is to ask questions. Leaders don't need all the answers. Curiosity is the third item in your Worthy to Lead Toolkit.

Tomas Chamorro-Premuzic wrote an article for *Harvard Business Review* in 2014 that showed curiosity is as important as intelligence. The risks when we let curiosity slip are fourfold. We can appear arrogant know-it-alls. We miss important information by making assumptions. We jump to solutions rather than keeping open to possible better outcomes. We increase our stress levels by carrying the weight of being across everything.

Curiosity enhances all aspects of our lives, not just at work. A woman in a program I ran in 2020 told me she was using questions with her teenage children in their afternoon conversations. After many years of grunts and single word answers, she began asking open questions followed by short silences. This allowed more time for her children to think and respond. She became more curious about what they said. My client was enjoying deeper conversations with her kids.

As she relayed her story, there were tears in her eyes and emotion in her voice. This was more important than being curious with her colleagues.

I know that every leader you like working with has made it look easy. They always have the answers you need. Why then would I tell you that leaders don't need to have all the solutions? If I haven't swayed you already, you might be beyond convincing. In every team development program I've run in the past seven years, people have told me the leaders they admire are positive, enthusiastic, and open to learning from their team. They're comfortable to say what they don't know and to take advice.

There are times when people in responsibility need to make rapid decisions, even when they don't have all the facts. These are the times when self-doubt can strike the hardest. It is when worthy self-talk is undermined. The inner voice says we are scared, ill-equipped and indecisive. But leaders can almost always take the time to gather more data before they act. Very few decisions are life and death at work, unless you're a first responder in an emergency. Curiosity is a heavy-duty power tool in our kit.

At the end of this chapter, I have listed questions you can use in various situations to enhance your curiosity and information gathering. Highlight your favourite question in each section. Practise using one or two questions and see what happens to your conversations. For an extra stretch, add a question of your own to each section. This will help you memorise the questions and you'll be more inclined to use them.

If you're worried people will judge you for asking questions, think of all the times in conferences, meetings, and workshops when someone apologises for asking an obvious question. Everyone else heaves a sigh of relief and they whisper to one another how thankful they are because they wanted to know the same thing.

Curiosity is often welcomed. Give questions a try and take the pressure off yourself to be the font of all knowledge. You're worthy of hearing and learning more.

Let's wrap this up

This chapter has provided you with a toolkit for your step up into leadership. You're now equipped with the three elements of leadership resilience and competence: connection, captivation, and curiosity.

It's possible you are still of the view that you don't know enough leaders with whom to connect. But you have a framework for addressing your concern. You have reviewed your level of captivation at work and you have an exercise to stretch you. Despite the misgiving that asking questions might annoy people, you've got a plan to practise being curious with some clever questions.

Set aside time in your diary to invite your list of leaders to coffee over the next three months.

Do the reflection exercise.

Identify at least three meetings to practise your favourite questions.

CHAPTER EIGHT: LEADERSHIP IS LONELY, ISN'T IT?

In the final chapter, the rubber hits the road. I will ask you to commit to yourself for the future and to form your **action plan.** It's the perfect follow-on from reviewing your commitment to your current job. Let's go.

Solution-focused question guide for leaders

1. Explore our intent
    - What would you like to accomplish?
    - What result are you trying to achieve?
    - What outcome would be ideal?
    - What's the best result we can aim for?
2. Explore what we know
    - What progress have you made so far?
    - What is working well right now?
    - What do you think is required of you?
    - What is stopping you?
3. Explore what's working
    - What's already going well?
    - What else could you do?
    - What has worked for you already? How could you do more of that?
    - How have you tackled this / a similar situation before?
    - Who do you know in the team who has encountered a similar situation?

4. Explore what's possible
   - What are your options?
   - Who else might be able to help?
   - What would happen if you did nothing?
   - What's the best / worst thing about that option?
5. Explore what's next
   - What do you think you need to do next?
   - What could be your first step?
   - How will you know when you have done it?
   - Is there anything else you can do?
   - Have we forgotten anything?
   - When are you going to start?

CHAPTER NINE

Commitment and clarity

You have reached the final chapter. At this point, things get real. This chapter is all about committing to yourself. It's time to take action.

Throughout the book, I have given you tools and tips to reframe your language and thoughts. In this final chapter, you will embed your worthy framework. Your framework will last beyond reading the book. You are a worthy woman. You are worthy of investing in yourself.

Our friend from Chapter One, Eckardt Tolle, said, 'Whatever you think the world is withholding from you, you are withholding from the world'. I'm not as erudite as Tolle. I would have said it's time to stop faffing around.

It's time for your **action plan**. A realistic plan to put in place and start working on straight away. If you don't, you risk putting this book back on the shelf to gather dust and leaving your development at the bottom of your priority list.

In his book, *Chatter*, Ethan Kross PhD, acclaimed psychologist and an authority on controlling the conscious mind, wrote about the hidden power of our inner voice. Kross shows how we can harness our internal chatter to live a healthier, more satisfying and more productive life.

I bet you talk to yourself. I also bet you've answered your own questions from time to time. I know I have—often with criticism. From now on, you need to talk to yourself as a worthy woman, as if you are encouraging your best friend.

Imagine your daughter or your best friend has come to you for advice about her professional and personal development. She explains the goals she has for self-improvement and education. She's frustrated and sad that she isn't making these things a higher priority.

She can't seem to crack through. Now imagine what you would say to her. Your kind, compassionate response is how your inner voice needs to talk to you.

In this chapter, I'll cover how to control and harness your self-talk so you can take action. I'll explain why you don't have to wait until you feel 100% confident before you start. I'll give you the tools to help to eliminate your excuses and put your development first.

Your 90-day plan

In the adulterated words of the Spice Girls, 'I'll tell you what I want, what I really, really want'. I want you to stabilise your self-talk and develop your 90-day plan. What do you want? And how do you imagine getting there?

When you don't know how to get your desires out of your head, you risk sitting on your hands. You feel wistful, not worthy. The way to get started evades you. The whole premise of this book and this chapter is how to move beyond those feelings. It's about how to step forward into action.

On how many New Year's Eves have you declared this to be the year you will lose five kilograms? A staggering 37% of people who made New Year's resolutions in 2019 wanted to lose weight, according to a survey by YouGov, an international research data and analytics group. Millions of people resolve to change their lives in some way at the start of every year. Then, they berate themselves a week, a month or a year later for not enacting it.

Have you ever done FebFast? FebFast is an annual challenge to 'pause for a cause' and give up alcohol, sugar or another vice for the month of February. Thousands of Australians do the program each year to raise funds for disadvantaged young people aged 12 to 25. Or what about Dry July? Dry July is an Australian fundraiser designed to encourage people to go alcohol-free for a month. The aim is to raise funds for people affected by cancer. Some people reduce their alcohol consumption long term or they give up drinking alcohol altogether.

Here's my point: when you plan a behaviour change or a goal in short cycles, you're geared for success. Shorter term plans increase your chances of achievement because it's not all or nothing. David Finkel, writing for *Fast Company* in his article, *The one-page cheat sheet to your most productive 90 days ever*, said,

> ... and while companies often sit down to draw up quarterly action plans, individuals rarely do. But they should. In fact, 90 days is the perfect unit of time to make headway on your big-picture goals— and to give them the focus they need, so you and your team don't get too overwhelmed.

The best bit? Rather than beating up on yourself at the end of the year for not doing what you planned, you get a specific and achievable task to do every three months.

At the end of the year, you've actioned four new things. I don't know about you, but that sounds like action, progress and success to me.

Are you convinced yet?

My friend Allison runs marathons. At 45 years of age, she's done a few now. Yet she didn't start running until she was in her mid-30s.

Allison didn't get up one morning, yawn, pop on her runners, and run 25 kilometres. Far from it. She started running one kilometre down her local rural road. Then five. Then ten. Until she cracked her first half marathon. If Allison had given herself a goal to run five kilometres per day, seven days per week, she would not have kept going. She would likely have hurt herself. Even though Allison is one of the most determined women I know, her inner voice would have had her demoralised.

At this point, you're either feeling energised and eager, or anxious and apprehensive. 'I've been here before,' I hear you say. 'It never works for me.' Well, hello inner voice talking in absolutes. There's the old external locus of control again. Remember her? We met her back in Chapter Five. It sounds like she believes your success is a result of factors beyond your control. Tell her to bugger off. You've got important planning to do.

 Exercise 12

Before you do anything else, use the questions below to set your intent and develop your plan for the next 90 days:

- What do you want to achieve? By when?
- Who should you tell about it?
- What will you notice when you have achieved it? (What will be different?)
- What's your first step and when will you do it?
- What resources or help do you need right now?
- What might be in your way?
- How will you get around this?

Some people find that doing the plan in one sitting works for them. Others need to come back to it after some thought. Do what works best for you. But don't mull over it for too long. Planning is about action. If you stall, it could mean your goal isn't easy, actionable, or trackable. Break it down. For example, instead of saying, 'Use the next 90 days to network with people who can be my mentors', make it easy and specific by saying, 'By this date, I will invite X to coffee to talk about my goals'.

Reframe your relationship with confidence

If 'Jill' had waited for confidence to arrive, she'd be lost and burned out. Jill joined my women's mentoring program. In this program, we use the 90-day planning tool. At the end of the initial group retreat and each subsequent session, members review and reflect on their plans. Each time Jill's group met, she created a single goal. As a senior executive and parent of two primary school aged children, Jill aimed to create more balance in her life. She started by dropping her working hours. Jill wasn't confident about the approach to her employer or the outcome. Yet she knew if she kept waiting, the opportunity to ask would pass. She risked feelings of overwhelm, more profound disengagement, and a complete loss of joy in her work.

Jill was brave, not confident. She was vulnerable. She decided to be direct and clear with her boss about how she felt, what she needed, and her goals. She also gave him the time frame she had for reaching her goals. Jill's honest approach to her boss paid off in spades. After reducing her working hours, Jill's next goal was to explore her new career choice. After almost two decades in one sector, she wanted a change. Her values analysis helped her see what she wanted most. From there, Jill's quarterly goal was to get an ABN and set up a consultancy as a new means of income. Her final goal was to set the date to leave her long-term job. At the time of writing this book, Jill had set the date to quit her job and had already managed several small consultancy projects.

If Jill had waited until she was confident, she'd still be working full-time and then some. She would not have established her business. Jill believes that had she not made these changes, she'd be struggling to get out of bed every morning.

Creator of *Women, work & success* (the first of its kind survey in Australia), Pollyanna Lenkic, says in her book, *Women & success*,

'Confidence is a wonderful thing to have; however, it is not essential to have it in place before stepping up'.

Like Lenkic, who is also a speaker, coach and mentor, I'm not saying confidence is a bad thing. Confidence IS cool. Just don't crave it. Get comfortable instead with being brave. Stretch yourself and do things regardless, even when you're not confident.

Dr Margie Warrell is renowned for her expertise in bravery. Warrell's thought leadership spans five bestselling books. Two of these, *Brave* and *You've got this!*, deal with building the courage to reach your aspirations even when confidence eludes you.

If you don't permit yourself to act until you feel confident, you risk waiting a long time. Life is one long (if you're lucky) experiment. Things change around you all the time. Like a goal shooter in a netball game, you need to be ready to shoot for the goal as soon as you catch the ball. If you wait for the perfect shot, the defence is on you. Be brave. Go for your ideal.

Confused? Until now, everything you've read, been told, or listened to has been about how women need to increase their confidence. If reading time is in short supply, grab Margie Warrell's short article from *Forbes*, *Don't wait for confidence: Start before you feel ready*. It will help you embed what you've learned here. It's a priority for you to change your relationship with confidence. Find 15 minutes to read the article even if it means reading it on the loo on your iPad. Whatever it takes.

CHAPTER NINE: COMMITMENT AND CLARITY

Eliminating excuses

It was the middle of the night. Tiana was breastfeeding her baby. She felt like the only person in the world who was awake at that time until a thought struck her: *You know what? On the other side of the planet, Angelina Jolie is probably sitting with her crying baby doing the same thing as me.* In that moment, Tiana realised she was like every other mum, even movie star mothers. She, too, could pursue her goals, on her terms.

Tiana held tight to her thought. A couple of years later, she invested in a coaching program to keep momentum in her work and studies as she undertook her PhD.

In her interview for this book, Tiana told me she wasn't sure how she would react to coaching with me. She said she used to 'bullshit' herself with excuses. 'I dressed it up as something else.' She talked about the self-limiting beliefs she held and her discovery that being content doesn't have to mean settling with what she already had. Tiana wanted more. She now knows this doesn't mean she's not happy. She still revels in gratitude. But she wants to learn more. To do and explore more. 'I've lost the apologetic and small me language. I have confidence that I am of value to other people. I'm so much more aware of my worth.'

Like Tiana, worthy women eliminate excuses. I don't need to tell you why this is important. I know you want to adopt worthy self-talk. I know you understand the value of planning in 90-day bursts; otherwise, you wouldn't have read this far.

Yet fear is what drives you to make excuses. Fear of loss. Fear of failure. Often, fear of success. And then, there's the fear of comparisons.

Like any coach will tell you, the work is yours to do. The powerful conversations you have with your coach are stimulating, challenging, and provocative. And none of that matters if you don't act on the goals you set in your sessions.

While I'm flattered you've read this far, my work is in vain if you don't act on what you've read. Not doing so means stalling your learning, career objectives, and joy in what you do for income. I'm sure that's not the role model you want to be for your daughters or sons or your younger colleagues. And it's not the person you want to face in the mirror each day. You either want to act worthy now or you don't.

Let's wrap this up

In this chapter, I have outlined how 90-day plans are practical tools for goal setting. I've shown you how confidence is a trickster to leave behind. Bravery serves you better. I've discussed excuses and why it's important to stop making them.

Your job is to think about how you feel about planning your goals quarterly. If you've been a person who plans annually or even further, this will be a shift.

You might also recoil at my suggestion that courage beats confidence. It flies in the face of things we learn from childhood. Messages suggesting that women need more confidence are insidious and everywhere. I hope I have convinced you that not waiting for certainty is a better option.

Now I'll offer you a series of questions to help you get over any excuses you might still be making.

It's time to go back over all the notes you've taken for each chapter in this book.

What's in your journal? Your notepad? What sticky notes have you stuck to the pages? What have you highlighted?

You will find what resonated most for you—the 'aha' moments. Listen to your gut and check your emotional responses to what you have written.

CHAPTER NINE: COMMITMENT AND CLARITY

Here are five questions to ask yourself about what you've recorded.

1. Choose your top three ideas to add to your next 90-day plan.
2. When you act on your plan, how will you feel?
3. Who else will notice?
4. What will they see?
5. How will you feel when they tell you what they see?

It's time to choose.

Conclusion

The L'Oréal Paris brand mission, 'Because you're worth it', is now 50 years old. Ilon Specht developed the tagline that is used in much of the cosmetics and haircare company's worldwide advertising. As a 23-year-old copywriter in New York, Specht worked for the advertising agency McCann. She could never have known that she would start an international campaign about something bigger than women believing in their own beauty.

The tagline has been translated into at least 40 languages. The L'Oréal website proclaims the company is still working towards a day when women hear the line 'Because you're worth it' and reply, '**We never doubted it for a moment**'.

Why has this branding touched such a nerve with women all over the world? Because although women know deep down that they are worth it, they often need reminding.

This book is your reminder. The entire manuscript is designed to be a reframe of your inner voice.

Worthy is a challenge to your usual practice of putting yourself second, third, or even last. Picking up this book and reading it has been an act of rebellion, if you will. GO YOU!

By reading this far, you've already invested in yourself. You're a woman with talents. Your aspirations matter. You don't need to remain wistful for all the things you thought you had missed out on in life. You're worth the investment of others. You're worth investing in you. **And it's never too late to start.**

Throughout the book, I have helped you reframe your thinking and your language. You are now equipped with worthy words to change your self-talk and the way you think about your development.

I contend that the more willing you are to open yourself to learning, the happier and more fulfilled you will be.

- You will have more options in your potential career plan, including a framework for leadership.
- You will make more money.
- You will expand your horizons exponentially.
- All by enacting your plan to invest more in yourself from today.

Keep your list of worthy words nearby for whenever you need to review them. Continue to add new words to describe your success.

I know I have raised some topics that made you squirm—that was deliberate. Just like exercise, you won't be stronger unless you are prepared to get uncomfortable and stretch.

What is the biggest obstacle ahead of you now? While you know all of the tips in this book, you might decide not to act on that knowledge. That's one choice. Or you could choose to implement what you know, inspire countless numbers of other women and girls, and create a fantastic legacy.

I know what outcome I'd choose for you.

If you doubt your ability to prioritise the actions in each chapter, I'll be frank. You are blocking your progress. Be accountable to yourself; use your diary or calendar to block out time every week to work on one of the chapters. Answer a question, complete an exercise, and read or watch one of the resources I have added for you.

Do this work step by step.

: CONCLUSION

You might like to team up with other readers. Share the book with friends and colleagues. Form a group to do the work together. What a powerhouse team you will be.

If you've got thoughts about the book, I'd love you to share them with me. Email me at hello@mareemcpherson.com.au with the subject line Worthy Woman. It will be great to hear from you.

Well, there it is then.

Everything I can think of from my life's experiences and those of my clients. All I know about how to feel worthy and how to act on that feeling.

I've spared you nothing. It's all here. My brain has been emptied.

Please notice the things that bring you joy. Pursue them with all of your heart and all of the means at your disposal. Why? Because **you are a Worthy Woman.**

Maree

Grow well, and go with love.

References

Allen, T. (2018, April 10). *How long is too long to stay in the same job and 3 huge risks for doing so*. LinkedIn. https://www.linkedin.com/pulse/how-long-too-stay-same-job-3-huge-risks-doing-so-terina-allen

AMP. (2019, March 28). *How our subconscious affects our attitude towards money*. https://www.amp.com.au/insights/manage-my-money/how-our-subconscious-affects-our-attitude-towards-money

Australian Government. (2008, May). *Financial literacy: Women understanding money*. Financial Literacy Foundation. https://www.financialcapability.gov.au/files/women-understanding-money.pdf

Ballard, J. (2020, January 3). *Exercising more and saving money are the most popular 2020 New Year's resolutions*. YouGov. https://today.yougov.com/topics/lifestyle/articles-reports/2020/01/02/new-years-resolutions-2020-health-finance

Brideson, R. J.. (2017, August). *Blind spots: How to uncover and attract the fastest emerging economy*. Wiley. https://www.wiley.com/en-au/Blind+Spots%3A+How+to+Uncover+and+Attract+the+Fastest+Emerging+Economy-p-9780730345404

Brockis, J. (2020). *Thriving mind: How to cultivate a good life*. Wiley.

Browne, M. (2012). *More money for shoes*. The Messenger Group.

Cain, S. (2013). *Quiet: The power of introverts in a world that can't stop talking* (0 ed.). Crown.

Cain, S. (2016). *Quiet power: The secret strengths of introverts*. Dial (Children).

Carter, C. (2020, September). *The 1-minute secret to forming a new habit*. TED. https://www.ted.com/talks/christine_carter_the_1_minute_secret_to_forming_a_new_habit/transcript?language=en

Chamorro-Premuzic, T. (2014, August 27). *Curiosity is as important as intelligence*. Harvard Business Review. https://hbr.org/2014/08/curiosity-is-as-important-as-intelligence

Condren, D. (2008). *Ambition is not a dirty word*. Crown.

Covey, S. (2012). *First things first* (Export edition ed.). Simon & Schuster.

Covey, S. R. (2020). *The 7 habits of highly effective people* (30th Anniversary Edition). Simon & Schuster.

Duckworth, A. (2018). *Grit: The power of passion and perseverance* (Illustrated ed.). Scribner.

Eagly, A. H. (2002, July). *Role congruity theory of prejudice toward female leaders*. PubMed. https://pubmed.ncbi.nlm.nih.gov/12088246/

Ernst & Young. (2013). *Women: The next emerging market*. https://assets.ey.com/content/dam/ey-sites/ey-com/en_gl/topics/growth/WomenTheNextEmergingMarket.pdf

Finkel, D. (2017, February 28). *The one-page cheat sheet to your most productive 90 days ever*. Fast Company. https://www.fastcompany.com/3068537/the-one-page-cheat-sheet-to-your-most-productive-90-days-ever

Ford, A. (2019, January 2). *Take 5: How to take charge of your professional development.* Kellogg Insight. https://insight.kellogg.northwestern.edu/article/take-5-how-to-take-charge-of-your-professional-development

Frankel, L. (2014). *Nice girls don't get the corner office: Unconscious mistakes women make that sabotage their careers (a NICE GIRLS book).* Little Brown.

Garner, J. (2017). *It's who you know: How a network of 12 key people can fast-track your success.* Wiley.

Grant, A. (2016). *Originals: How non-conformists move the world.* Penguin Books.

Grant, A. (2018). *WorkLife with Adam Grant: A TED original podcast.* TED. https://www.ted.com/podcasts/worklife

Grant, A. (2021). *Think again: The power of knowing what you don't know.* WH ALLEN.

Green, S. (2021, January 6). *10 ways to support and empower the women in your life this year.* SHE DEFINED. https://shedefined.com.au/life/10-ways-to-support-and-empower-the-women-in-your-life-this-year/

HBR. (2018, April 5). *Career Transitions.* Harvard Business Review. https://hbr.org/podcast/2018/04/career-transitions

Hollis, R. (2019). *Girl, stop apologizing: A shame-free plan for embracing and achieving your goals.* Harpercollins Leadership.

Hopper, E. (2020, July 3). *How volunteering can help your mental health.* Greater Good. https://greatergood.berkeley.edu/article/item/how_volunteering_can_help_your_mental_health

Johnson, W. (2016). *Disrupt yourself: Putting the power of disruptive innovation to work.* Bibliomotion.

Khoo, V. (2011, November 24). *The truth about the new business women's networks.* The Sydney Morning Herald. https://www.

smh.com.au/business/small-business/the-truth-about-the-new-business-womens-networks-20111124-1nvqd.html

Kross, E. (2021). *Chatter: The voice in our head, why it matters, and how to harness it.* Crown.

Lamson, M. (2018, June 7). *You're not burnt-out. You're bored-out.* Inc. https://www.inc.com/melissa-lamson/8-ways-to-conquer-bore-out.html

Lenkic, P. (2015). *Women & success: Redefining what matters most at home, at work and at play.* BookPOD.

McKay, A. (2021). *You don't need an MBA: Leadership lessons that cut through the crap.* Major Street Publishing.

McNulty, A. (2018, September 3). *Don't underestimate the power of women supporting each other at work.* Harvard Business Review. https://hbr.org/2018/09/dont-underestimate-the-power-of-women-supporting-each-other-at-work

McPherson, M. (2017). *Cutting through the grass ceiling: Women creating possibility in regional Australia.* BookPod.

McPherson, M. (2020, November 4). *Afternoon with an author - Dr Jenny Brockis.* Maree McPherson. https://www.mareemcpherson.com.au/shop/dr-jenny-brockis

Miller, B. (n.d.). *Locus of control, learned helplessness, and the tyranny of choice.* Khan Academy. Retrieved 2 June 2021, from https://www.khanacademy.org/test-prep/mcat/individuals-and-society/attributing-behavior-to-persons-or-situations/v/personal-control-locus-of-control-learned-helplessness-and-the-tyranny-of-choice

Obama, M. (2021). *Becoming.* Delacorte Press.

Orman, S. (2018). *Women & money (revised and updated)* (Revised, Updated ed.). Random House.

Pape, S. (2016). *The barefoot investor* (1st ed.). Wiley.

REFERENCES

Pearce, N., & Palmer, P. J. (2019). *The purpose path: A guide to pursuing your authentic life's work*. St. Martin's Essentials.

Rizvi, J. (2018, December 3). *Not just lucky*. Penguin Books Australia.

Rothschild, H. (2016, April 5). *Is knowing when to go the ultimate leadership challenge?* LinkedIn. https://www.linkedin.com/pulse/knowing-when-go-ultimate-leadership-challenge-henriette-rothschild/

Sandberg, S. (2015). *Lean in: Women, work, and the will to lead*. Random House UK.

Stewart, C. (2020, November 21). 3 consequences when introverted women leaders put on an extroverted persona. LinkedIn. https://www.linkedin.com/pulse/3-consequences-when-introverted-women-leaders-put-carol/

Springer. (n.d.). *Journal of happiness studies*. Retrieved 2 June 2021, from https://www.springer.com/journal/10902/

Totenberg, N. (2020, September 19). *A 5-decade-long friendship that began with a phone call*. NPR. https://www.npr.org/2020/09/19/896733375/a-five-decade-long-friendship-that-began-with-a-phone-call

Warrell, M. (2015). *Brave: 50 everyday acts of courage to thrive in work, love and life*. Wiley.

Warrell, M. (2020a). *You've got this!: The life-changing power of trusting yourself* (1st ed.). Wiley.

Warrell, M. (2020b, February 24). *Don't wait for confidence: Start before you feel ready*. Forbes. https://www.forbes.com/sites/margiewarrell/2020/02/24/dont-wait-for-confidence-its-over-rated/?sh=5a65b24749b1

Willyerd, K., Mistick, B., & Grenny, J. (2016). *Stretch: How to future-proof yourself for tomorrow's workplace*. Wiley.

Witherspoon, R. (2017, September 5). *We have to change the idea that a woman with ambition is only out for herself.* Glamour. https://www.glamour.com/story/reese-witherspoon-october-2017-cover-interview

Zenger, J., & Folkman, J. (2013, September 11). *Nice or tough: Which approach engages employees most?* Harvard Business Review. https://hbr.org/2013/09/nice-or-tough-what-engages-emp

Zenger, J., & Folkman, J. (2017, May 9). *How to improve at work when you're not getting feedback.* Harvard Business Review. https://hbr.org/2017/05/how-to-improve-at-work-when-youre-not-getting-feedback

מכללת תלמוד להתפתחות אישית. (2017, February 21). *Everyone needs a coach - Bill Gates & Eric Schmidt.* YouTube. https://www.youtube.com/watch?v=8R1pHd4niLI

www.ingramcontent.com/pod-product-compliance
Lightning Source LLC
Chambersburg PA
CBHW051131160426
43195CB00014B/2431